ALSO BY JOHN GIERACH

Even Brook Trout Get the Blues

Where the Trout Are All as Long as Your Leg

Sex, Death, & Fly-Fishing

The View from Rat Lake

Fly Fishing Small Streams

Trout Bum

Flyfishing the High Country

Illustrated by Glenn Wolff

S I M O N & S C H U S T E R
New York London Toronto
Sydney Tokyo Singapore

JOHN GIERACH

Dances
with
Trout

SIMON & SCHUSTER
Rockefeller Center
1230 Avenue of the Americas
New York, New York 10020

Copyright © 1994 by John Gierach

SIMON & SCHUSTER and colophon are registered trademarks
of Simon & Schuster Inc.

Designed by Karolina Harris
Manufactured in the United States of America

10   9   8   7   6   5   4   3   2

Library of Congress Cataloging-in-Publication Data
Gierach, John, date.
Dances with trout / John Gierach.
p.   cm.
1. Fly fishing—United States—Anecdotes.
2. Hunting—United States—Anecdotes.
3. Gierach, John, date. I. Title.
SH456.G55 1994
799.1'755—dc20   93-34931 CIP
ISBN 0-671-77924-9

CONTENTS

The world punishes us for taking it too seriously as well as for not taking it seriously enough.

—JOHN UPDIKE

1

The Lake

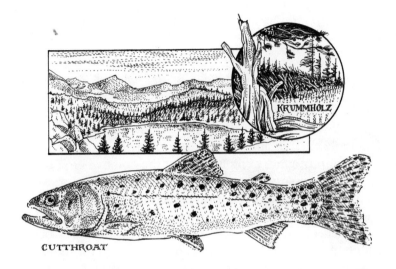

CUTTHROAT

One summer, A. K. Best, Larry Pogreba and I walked up into a high mountain valley we know of to find and fish a certain alpine lake. The most recent report we had on it was ten years old but, back then at least, it was supposed to have some big cutthroat trout. This is a remote lake that's not fished much, which naturally gets you to thinking.

I'd never been to this lake, or to any of the half dozen other lakes and hanging puddles on that far southwest ridge, even though I've been fishing, hiking and hunting in the valley off and on for somewhere between fifteen and twenty years and had, only the summer before, systematically fished the entire length of the stream from the last paved county road up to the headwaters.

I'll admit right here that this was more of a writing than a completely honest sporting proposition. I had in mind one of those gradual revelation numbers: Fishing the stream yard by yard, mile by mile, the details would build up novelistically until finally I would catch the last tiny cutthroat trout sucking snowflies from the lip of the glacier and there'd be this vague but satisfying sense of completion, which I would somehow get down on paper. I had it all worked out. Kevin Costner would play me in the movie version, *Dances with Trout.*

I did manage to fish the whole stream in a single season, all fifteen miles of it. If I remember right, it took ten separate trips between the end of runoff in June and the first good snow in September. Once or twice I went alone, but more often I was with A.K., Mike Price or Ed Engle.

Oddly enough, I never got close to anything especially literary or profound, except maybe at the point where I forgot why I was doing it. There was still an amorphous sense of purpose that I liked. It was more serious than play, less serious than work (a distinction made more subtle by the fact that I usually work harder playing than I do working), but in the end it became one of those things you do for the sheer hell of it, just so you can say you did it.

Also, I caught lots of fish. That's just good, clean fun but, as often as it happens, it still seems like proof of something. The trout takes the fly, the line tightens and it's like I was blind, but now I see. I have to admit there are days when I fish as a conscious act of revolution, but the days when I fish for no apparent reason at all are usually better.

I thought about keeping a journal, but when it came right down to it I didn't. For one thing, I didn't want to be bothered scribbling when I could be fishing. For another, I knew I'd be happier relying on my recollections because the memory of a fisherman is more like fiction than journalism, that is, it doesn't ignore the facts, but it's not entirely bound by them, either.

When I finally did catch what had to be the last cutthroat

from the last trickle deep enough to hold one, I thought, Okay, *there*. Then I started thinking about that lake up on the ridge and the rumors about big trout. The lesson about writing had something to do with endings: like maybe they don't really exist in nature.

That was the summer that the idea of minimum flows lower down on the same drainage floated to the surface once again, as it does about every five years or so. By now all the studies have been done and the experts tend to agree: Water quality, biomass, species diversity—it's all there. Just add a proper, minimum winter flow—enough to let the larger trout live until spring—and you'll have one hell of a trout stream.

This is something a handful of us locals have been kicking around for a couple of decades now, first as part of Trout Unlimited, then as I don't know what. At one point some people started referring to us as the TLO (the Trout Liberation Organization) but that didn't stick because right about then it was becoming clear that terrorism wasn't really very funny. I suggested the National Riffle Association, but in the end we didn't need a name because we weren't an organization in the usual sense. I think we realized it was better to remain a nameless, unorganized handful of people with a more or less common vision so that the occasional good idea wouldn't have to undergo surgery by a committee.

So for quite a while now we've been trying first one tactic and then another, keeping the idea of minimum flows alive because it might eventually catch on and looking for the chink in the state and local bureaucracies that would allow everyone in power to gracefully do the right thing.

The main problem is, it's hard to get used to the level of discourse you're involved in. When you go to a bureaucrat with an idea, he looks you in the eye, smiles warmly and thinks, "Is there anything in this for me and, if not, what's the quickest way to get rid of this guy?" When you approach a politician, he thinks, "How can I be simultaneously for and against this?" not realizing that by being on both sides of a fight he'll eventually beat himself up.

When you start talking about putting water back into a stream because it belongs there, you're screwing around with one of the oldest Old World artifacts on this continent. Water law here dates back roughly to the introduction of the horse into North America. By now it's become pretty well fossilized.

The stretch of stream I was fishing that summer was at the top end of the drainage, in a wilderness area, above the dams, ditches, headgates and all the other plumbing by which too much water was being stolen from the stream and by which also reasonable people could put some back. Not all of it—just enough for the fish to breathe.

That upper fork is not exactly untouched, but it's still nicely out of the loop. If you walk far enough upstream, you can literally, that is, *physically,* leave the argument behind, and that's . . . what? Let's say, liberating. Or let's say that, without diminishing the importance of the environmental issue at hand, it can give you a larger perspective: Left to themselves, things are as they are because they couldn't be any other way, right?

One day, in the course of doing a lunch with a guy who might have been made to see minimum flows in the lower stream working to his advantage, the man asked me, "What is it you really want?" assuming, of course, that what I *told* him I wanted was a smokescreen behind which a hidden agenda was advancing unseen.

I can often wait out a trout, but I tend to lose patience quickly with humans, so I slipped and said, "What I really want is for us to disassemble enough of modern technological culture that we can become a nation of agrarian anarchist, gourmet hunter/gatherer, poet/sportsmen." That may or may not have been a mistake, but it was therapeutic.

That was also the year I began to get interested in the concept of bioregionalism: the idea that your coherent, familiar, natural habitat is much more important to you in the long run than political boundaries, not to mention much harder to define. I guess I'd known that instinctively all along, but it was only recently that I'd discovered the label and the small, backwater political movement that comes with it.

So as an exercise in visualization, I asked myself, honestly now, ignoring meaningless designations like United States of America, Colorado, Boulder County, St. Vrain Valley School District or an arbitrarily selected stretch of trout stream, where do you feel you belong? I started with the places where the water is cold enough to support trout and where I know enough to dress for the weather, overlaid the ranges of mule deer, snowshoe hares and the species of grouse I know how to hunt, added spruce, fir and pine trees and the few edible mushrooms I can identify.

It became obvious that I was fundamentally at home either in one small drainage in the Colorado Rockies or anywhere in the northern third of North America. I found that helpful. Everyone should have a rough idea where home is.

The fork of the stream and the rumored cutthroat lake are in one of those classically beautiful, high, wide but somehow still intimate valleys in the Colorado Rockies, and parts of it are nicely inaccessible. First there's an hour and a half's worth of jarring, slamming bad road. Then, at the road's end, there's a pretty good uphill hike past the stretch of stream that's fished by the four-wheel brigade. After several miles the trout change from brookies to cutthroats, some of which get unusually large for that kind of high, sparse water.

The stream itself is small, cold, steep, deep in places, shallow and braided in others and jumbled with boulders and the bleached trunks of fallen spruce and fir trees. It's mostly in forest, so the water is nicely shaded, but the dense spruce and fir needles will grab your flies and leaders on careless back casts and hold on to them like Velcro.

This does not make for graceful fly-fishing. You scramble

over rocks and rotting logs, make short, choppy casts and lose flies to snags but, because most fishermen won't put themselves through this—let alone walk that far to do it—the hardest spots give up the best trout.

This is the kind of fine little creek that grabs and holds your attention, and it's hard enough to get to in its own right that it can keep you from exploring further. But I was honestly curious about the lake, and also a little worried that someone would eventually ask me about it, based on the assumption that I've been kicking around the area for two decades and must know it like the proverbial back of my hand. I'd have to admit the truth, they'd say something like, "Oh, so in all that time you never actually went *all the way back in there*," and that would sting.

The three of us hiked in from the end of the four-wheel-drive road and, although we had a destination in mind, we couldn't help stopping here and there along the creek to catch, admire and release a few trout. I directed Larry to some good spots I'd discovered the year before, and in fifteen minutes he'd landed a couple of fourteen-inch cutthroats.

"Jeeze," he said, "I didn't know they got this big up here."

I beamed, proud of myself, even though he'd have found the fish easily enough without my help, and A.K. mumbled, "Just keep it to yourself, okay?"

There was talk of keeping a few trout to eat, but it was early in the day and we had a long walk ahead of us. The fish might have gotten a little funky by the time we got them home, and there are few things worse than wild trout that could have been fresh, but aren't.

Then we found the little feeder creek that was supposed to come from the lake in question and started climbing. The directions were good so far; there was the old skid road, the ruined bridge and the advice, "It's the first big feeder you come to." The slope was steep, the air was thin. A.K. and I began to plod while Larry pulled out ahead and found some perfect, doorknob-sized Boletus mushrooms that he stuffed into his fly vest.

Not far past the mushrooms we came out of the tall, shady spruce/fir forest into the open. Larry charged ahead, but A.K. and I stopped there for a few minutes to reacclimate. To me, coming out of the dark timber at high altitude is like walking out of a movie matinee into a hard, bright summer afternoon. The eyes squint, vision swims and you stoop a little so as not to bump your head on the sky.

After some more hard going we did, in fact, come to a lake, but it was too shallow, too small, obviously fishless and couldn't have been *the* lake.

We rested for a few minutes, then consulted the compass and map. We should have done this earlier, but the guy with the decade-old fishing report was the one who'd said to follow that particular feeder creek and we'd trusted his memory. He'd been wrong, which cast something of a shadow on the whole enterprise.

None of us are great at orienteering, but it became clear that we were too far east, although it wasn't clear *how* far. So we worked our way roughly west along the rock shelves, boulder fields and miniature knee- to chest-high spruce groves, finally coming to a pair of large pools on a feeder creek that weren't on the map and, a hundred feet farther up, a pair of lakes that were.

Okay, now we knew where we were. The shapes and placement of the lakes and the prominent landmarks were unmistakable. Where we needed to be was a mile or so farther south by southwest and a few hundred feet higher. We looked in that direction and there stood an enormous, ominous-looking crag of rock, on the other side of which would be the lake we wanted.

Someone dug out a watch to check the time. It was too late to do anything but fish the lakes at hand for half an hour and then head out at a quick pace if we wanted to negotiate that four-wheel-drive road with any daylight left. That seemed like a good idea, since we'd wrecked a tire on the way in and were running on the spare. We were using Larry's Suburbillac, an ingenious homemade Suburban/Cadillac/pop-up camper hybrid that I won't try to describe here. It's a solid vehicle, but too odd-looking to instill a lot of confidence in skeptical passengers.

We fished the larger of the two lakes for a while, mostly as an exercise. There were no rises, no fish cruising the shallows. In terms of vegetation, aquatic insects and trout, it looked as sterile as a stone toilet bowl. Still, after all that walking it was fun to stand and make long, straight casts out onto the pretty water.

These sparse, high lakes can and do winterkill, leaving them with no life that would interest a guy who'd carried a fly rod six or seven miles and two thousand feet up. Then again, bodies of water just like this have been known to look fishless, but hold a handful of five-pound cutthroats that you might locate after two days of watching and random casting, but not in half an hour. So if someone asks me if there are trout in Such-and-Such Lake, I'll have to answer, in all honesty, "I don't know, I didn't see any." But, I can add silently, I *did* go look.

We were at roughly 11,000 feet, where the air is cool, thin and dizzyingly clear, even to westerners. The larger of the two lakes was set smack against the base of a nameless (by the map) 12,400-foot peak on the Continental Divide with other sharp summits reaching past 13,000 visible along the ridge to the north and west. Looking down valley to the northeast, we could see the nearly flat-topped, almost vertical escarpment that forms the north wall of the gorge. This is a natural barrier to the elk herds that move down and east in the fall so that, although the little valley is rich in other kinds of game, elk are rare.

Fooling around with maps of the area, I once determined that from almost any good, high vantage point in the upper valley one can see something like ninety square miles of rock, tundra, forests, lakes and trout streams. On site, it doesn't seem anywhere near that big.

The lake itself was clear at the shallow end, but the deep hole on the far side was a milky blue-green color from the little glacier to the south. Patches of the nearer snowfields had a slight pinkish cast caused by a kind of wind-borne snow mold. This stuff is said to taste like watermelon, but it's also supposed to be either a neurotoxin or a psychedelic, depending on which survivor you talk to.

This is the area that lies between timberline (above which trees won't grow tall and straight) and treeline (above which trees won't grow at all). It's called *krummholz:* a German word meaning "crooked wood."

Some of the small, gnarled trees here are ancient, though how ancient I can only guess. The oldest known individual living things on the planet are some bristlecone pines living in California in terrain something like this. They're said to be well over four thousand years of age. A local botanist says that in this area krummholz spruce several hundred years old may have a trunk diameter of only four inches, and there are old trees here that are more than a foot across at the base.

It's trees like this that inspired the art of bonsai growing in China and Japan. The bonsai masterpieces (outrageous, shallowly potted trees, some of which are hundreds of years old) symbolize great strength, wiry toughness, stillness, patience, eccentricity, adaptation, harmonious balance, goofiness and the venerable wisdom that can come from old age: all the attributes enlightened humans can take from wildness if they're smart enough to pay attention.

Of course they also symbolize how an honest love of nature can turn on itself. According to bonsai grower Peter Chin, many mountainous areas of Japan were stripped of their beautiful, naturally dwarfed trees by bonsai collectors long ago. To see them now you have to go to the cities. And this from a culture that has always based its art and philosophy on a close harmony with the natural world.

It's interesting that, because we Americans have loved nature less and for a shorter time, these lovely little trees (which are, after all, too small for lumber) still grow in our mountains. In this kind of terrain you see examples of two classic bonsai styles—*kengai* (cascade) and *fukinagashi* (windswept). Digging one to transplant would be three times harder than grunting up there to fish, and it's illegal anyway.

No trout were going to come from the lake in front of us, that much was clear, and as we were reeling in and heading back to where we'd piled our day packs, A.K. said, "It's yet another success. We said we were going fishing and that's what we did."

A thousand feet below, down in the tall, straight trees, we could see a small, nameless lake where I'd caught cutthroat trout as long as sixteen inches that year, although we wouldn't have time to fish for them now. From that vantage point we could also pick out the easy, more or less direct route to the lake we'd set out for that morning, and we filed that for future reference.

The sun was far to the west, a little over an hour from dusk. The shadows across the valley behind us were long and pointed—olive and honey-colored on the bare rocks, almost black down in the trees and dull silver on the lower lake. The peaks on the far ridge were starting to get an amber glow. All in all, it was a far better place to be than a bar or a gas station when a flopped expedition begins to take on that aimless feeling.

It was going to be a long, fast walk out, so we broke down our rods, shouldered our packs and had that brief consultation that becomes standard with middle-aged outdoorsmen who have come to know of each other's old injuries:

"How's your back?"

"Fine, how's your foot?"

"Okay, how's your knee?"

"Sore, but it's all downhill from here."

2

Quitting Early

*T*he deal was this: Most of the river was private through this stretch, or, I should say, the surrounding land was private, since Montana's enlightened Stream Access Law allows you to walk and fish on any river as long as you stay below the high-water line.

Still, some of this water would have involved a really long, hard hike from the nearest public access except that one landowner allows fishermen to park and get in on his land for a fee of three dollars. You have to know where the turnoff is, but once you get down to the river there's a large, hand-painted sign that explains the procedure in detail, complete with some interesting spelling errors.

You get an envelope from an old, tin tackle box on a stump, stick three dollars in it, write your license number on the outside and put it in the slot on a large, handmade strong-box that's too big and heavy to steal.

There's no one around, it's an honor system, but before you even think of not doing it, you come to the part of the instructions saying that nonpayers will be banned. Actually it says, "NONE PAYERS WILL BE BAND," which somehow makes the point with even more authority.

There were some other fishermen rigging up there, and one of them came over and asked me if it was true what he'd heard about the old man who owned the place: that he'd drive down from the hills in the evening, check the en-velopes against the license plates and go after cheaters with a shotgun.

"You bet," I said, although I'd never met the old man or even heard the story before. Everywhere you go in the Rocky Mountain West you'll hear tales of crazy old landowners with guns. More of them are true than you might suspect.

My partner and I had floated a different stretch of the same river with a guide that morning. We'd caught lots of trout and then had a great, leisurely meal at a little roadhouse nearby where it was okay to wear waders inside but, "please, no cleats." Before our guide headed back to town, he told us about the strongbox, the three dollars and all; said we should fish there as long as we were this close and asked me not to write about where it was. So I haven't. Okay, Tom?

He said, "You want to fish river-left this evening and river-right if you go back there in the morning." River-left is to your left as you look downstream, which is how Mackenzie boat guides view the world. It would also be the shady bank at that time of day.

You had your choice of sides because there was a rickety old one-lane wooden bridge down there. The river was way too wide, deep and fast to wade across.

Lunch was long and slow, as I said, but we were still at the bridge with our three dollars paid by early afternoon. Our guide had blasted back to town in what seemed like a big hurry. Some of these guys tow their Mackenzie boats faster than I'd drive a Porsche on those twisty, two-lane roads, but you hardly ever see them in a ditch, so they must know what they're doing.

This was in mid-August. The day was hot and bright, and it was going to be quite a few hours before evening when things should pick up. So we rigged up slowly to kill time: stretching leaders, checking perfectly good knots, adjusting reel drags that didn't need adjusting, carefully smoothing every last wrinkle out of the wader socks and drinking our canteens dry; hydrating, so we wouldn't have to carry water.

We even stopped and talked to another fisherman who was mad because he hadn't been able to get any good pancakes. He'd eaten breakfast in a dozen cafés and restaurants around there, but the pancakes were always too thick and fluffy. "Now any good pancake," he said, "is thin and firm, right?"

We listened to this guy for longer than we normally would have, but even at that, we were on the river by three o'clock and it would probably be seven or later before anything really happened.

The fishing was refreshingly slow-paced after the frantic morning in the Mack boat. We split up and worked the pocket water near shore, pretty much ignoring the great, roaring main channel out in the middle. I was using a size sixteen dry caddis fly with a little Hares Ear nymph on a short dropper, a rig I like because you seem to be casting a dry fly like a proper sporting gentleman, even though you're hooking most of your trout on the nymph.

I also like it because it goes against the still popular myth that the only way to catch trout in these big, western rivers is to dredge the bottom with a huge weighted stonefly.

The fishing was slow, but it felt good to be wading in cold water under a hot sun, and now and then—maybe once every half hour—you'd hook a nice, fat rainbow that just couldn't wait for the evening hatch. It was dreamy enough to let you stop and look at the birds and maybe scan the hillsides for game, but you'd get just enough strikes to keep your mind from wandering to far-off things like home, work and the future. This is probably how a grazing deer feels: happily lazy, but still alert and in the moment.

Things did pick up a little toward evening. A few caddis flies began to come off and some trout started rising. When I finally broke the nymph off on a fish, I clipped the rest of the dropper off and fished with the dry fly alone. When I lost the little Elk Hair Caddis to another trout, I tied a fresh fly onto a new, slightly heavier tippet, squared my shoulders, readjusted my hat and got serious for a while.

This is exactly how a summer day on a big, western river is supposed to go: hot fishing in the morning, petering off to a midday during which you can either pound up the odd trout if you want to or take a nap, then slipping into an evening rise that will likely last until past dark.

By the time the sun was completely off the river, I'd landed half a dozen good trout on the fresh caddis fly, including two rainbows that would have gone around sixteen inches. I'd started the morning with a couple of good fish on a dry fly, so this seemed to be an appropriate place to quit. When I released that last big trout I remember thinking the first one I'd caught that day had been thirteen or fourteen hours before and that I'd lost track of them in between. I also remember being a little tired.

Sure, the fish would keep feeding and there'd be enough light to see my caddis fly for another half hour or so. For that matter, with stars and a quarter moon, a guy could tie on a #10 Royal Wulff and go on for half the night, but toward the end of a long day that's gone well I now often ask myself things like, Just how many fish do you have to catch?

No, I'm not always this laid back, but we'd been out for several days, so the initial adrenaline rush had subsided. I've always enjoyed that moment on a trip when the long haul comes into view—plenty of water to fish, plenty of time— and it no longer feels like a suicide mission.

I got up on a faint fisherman's trail winding through the sage and headed back. When I passed my partner I yelled down to him, "I'll see you at the truck."

"They're really rising down here," he said.

Back at the parking lot I set up the camp stove on the tailgate and made coffee. There'd been six or eight trucks and jeeps there when we went out, now there were three. Right next to me the guy who'd asked me about the landowner there hours before was pulling off his neoprene waders and wringing out his wet long johns and socks. He sniffed his underwear tentatively and said, half to me, half to himself, "Can't tell if this is river water or condensation."

He seemed pensive, as though he was coming to the realization many of us have reached over the last few years, namely that neoprenes—expensive waders that make you wet whether they leak or not—are probably an elaborate practical joke.

"Got time for some coffee?" I asked.

"I'll have a beer," he said, reaching for his cooler, "but I sure as hell have time. The guy I'm with will probably be out there till midnight."

I said, "Yeah, my partner will be out late, too, if only because he knows I quit early."

The guy laughed knowingly at that, and then we ran through the usual fisherman's business. First things first: How'd you do today? (We'd both lost count of trout caught and were satisfied.) Where else have you been in the last few days? How was the fishing? What flies did you use? How do you like that rod? And, by the way, what's your name?

Shortly after dark two guys came off the water, derigged quickly and without much comment and drove off in the third pickup. Half a mile down the dirt track they turned left onto the county road, in the direction of that little roadhouse. I caught myself wondering what time they stopped serving burgers there and fought the impulse to look at my watch.

Checking the time when the time doesn't matter always makes me feel compulsive.

The river had gotten louder—as rivers do on those clear, western nights—and we watched what we could see of it for a while without talking. What we could see was a wide black stripe in a bumpy gray landscape.

There are times when I really enjoy that: coming back a little early, getting out of the waders, brewing coffee, unwinding and knowing that my friend is still out there in the dark somewhere, probably—presumably—landing a few more trout. It's like figuring the bats must be out because of the time of day and the season, even though you can't actually see them.

I knew what he'd say when he finally dragged in. He'd have hammered them, big ones, starting ten minutes after I left. (That might sound suspicious, but it would be true—the big trout really do move after dark, and the guys who stay late on the water usually get some.) He'd tell me this in a slightly accusatory tone because my quitting early would have offended him in some way. In the final analysis, he thinks I lack a certain grim determination when it comes to trout fishing.

And he's right, I do. In fact, it took me a long time to get to where I could fish as if it mattered, but not as if I was at war with the trout. I had to work at it at first, but now I prefer it that way.

So, he can't understand why I'd quit when there was even one more trout to be stuck and I can't understand why he can never quite get enough, but I guess it's one of those things that, in the long course of a friendship, seems to matter less and less. I mean, no one understands everything, right?

And it could be a lot worse. Over the years I've fished with frustrated drill sergeants who absolutely have to be in charge of everything; phony experts who always have to be right; competitors who keep score so they can win and you can lose; headhunters whose biggest trout has to be longer than yours for reasons that seem suspiciously Freudian and so on. In the grand scheme of things, someone who makes you wait at the truck for an hour or so is nothing.

The other man and I were still watching the river. I'd finished my coffee and accepted one of his cold beers, which tasted so wonderful I almost fell off the tailgate. My friend out on the water had taught me that years ago: When you're tired, have a cup of coffee first so you can stay awake to enjoy the beer. The night had turned cold and I'd put on a sweater.

I said, "This guy you're fishing with, have you known him long?"

"Oh, God," he said, "I've known him for years. He can be an asshole at times, but we get along."

3

Fool Hens

*J*ust over twenty years ago, not long after I'd moved to Colorado from the Midwest, an old guy who lived up in the mountains told me that porcupines were great survival food. They don't taste very good (they're strong and greasy) and they are, as you'd expect, a little ticklish to clean, but a person lost and alone without tools or weapons can bag one with a rock. One thing I'd noticed right off about the Rocky Mountains was that there was always one of those handy.

Fantastic, I thought. This was exactly the kind of thing I'd come west to learn.

Second only to the porcupine, this guy said, was the blue grouse. You needed a firearm of some kind (or at least a bow or slingshot), but the blues, when you found them, would just sit in trees looking at you stupidly and you could pick them off easily. Sometimes they wouldn't even seem to mind the shot or a fallen comrade and you could knock off a couple. (You always start with the birds on the lower branches, the guy said.) And they tasted a lot better than porcupine, too.

This guy referred to blue grouse as fool hens, which I later learned is what most natives out here call them.

I may not have known much when I was in my early twenties, but I'd been brought up right and did know that grouse are properly shot on the wing with light double-barrel shotguns, preferably over dogs. I didn't say anything to the old guy, though, because I understood that I was talking survival (not sport) with a by God, authentic Colorado mountain man, or at least that's how I saw it then. I was, however, happy to learn that there were grouse in the woods.

In fact, there are lots of them, each different species neatly adapted to its own type of habitat to the apparent end that there should be grouse wherever possible.

Most of the grouse are described in the books as locally common with some seasonal movement, which, as far as I can tell, means either they're there or they're not. So western grouse hunters do a lot of walking and the kind of bird they're after determines the countryside they hike through.

Ptarmigan live at or above treeline, in the boulder fields dotted with gnarled, stunted tree islands and on up into the bare, exposed, jagged alpine tundra. The country is high (usually well above ten thousand feet), open, enormous, vertical, dramatic, at least chilly in the fall, if not downright cold, and always subject to storms.

A geologist friend tells me the rocks here are the oldest in the Rockies, pushed up from far below by the forces of plate tectonics, but in another way this is geologically new country. The peaks are sharp and fresh, not yet polished by the elements. Rocks regularly break off and rattle down the scree slopes (that's the distant clacking sound you keep hearing), and the boulders you walk through look freshly cleaved with sharp, clean edges, many so new that lichens haven't taken hold yet.

You can walk many miles here looking for a few spooky, well-camouflaged birds, and in some places you had to walk miles to get there in the first place, all uphill, of course. The air is thin, the slopes steep and the footing in these loose, young mountains can be uncertain. Rock-hopping with a shotgun and backpack requires balance, foresight and good depth perception. In most places, if you lose your balance you won't fall far, but you'll land hard on sharp stuff. You learn to go at your best, safe pace, even if the guy you're with is dancing out ahead like a goat.

Grouse plumage is cryptic, as the ornithologists say—that is, they take on the coloration of their environment—and ptarmigan are the best. In winter they turn pure white, like a snowshoe hare. In hunting season they're the overall golden tan color of, let's say, clover honey spread on whole wheat toast, laced with irregular patches of chocolate and black on their backs—like lichen-covered rocks—and they're white underneath. The white underparts break up whatever you might see of the bird silhouette and, since they reflect light from below, they don't throw shadows, which is kind of eerie.

Ptarmigan don't so much run and freeze through the boulder fields, it's more like they dissolve and reform. Even when they move, they look less like grouse and more like that swimming vision you can get from high altitude and more exertion than you're used to.

Ptarmigan back and flank feathers make good hackles for certain nymphs and soft hackled wet flies, and those mottled, honey and brown feathers are the perfect legs for golden stonefly nymphs.

I think about trout flies here because cutthroats are sometimes found in the small, cold lakes around treeline, and the short ptarmigan season in September runs right through some of the last and the best of the high lake fishing. Since both of these involve going a long way at some expense in physical effort, I tend to fall into the cast and blast mode, clumsily lugging a fly rod and shotgun along with all the other stuff I need for a day in the high mountains.

I say "clumsily" because I don't have one of those efficient little pack rods that break down into many pieces for easy carrying, although every time I do this I swear I'll buy one the minute I get back.

The cast and blast, fish and fowl trip doesn't always work, but it's glorious when it does. The last time out, Larry, Steve Peterson, Dutch the pointer and I hiked up into a high cirque above treeline where ptarmigan and cutthroats were said to live.

To make a long story short, the ptarmigan were there and it was amazing that we found them: a single, large flock dodging like hallucinations through vast boulder fields. The bag limit is three each. We got five among us.

Then we went to look at the lakes, but the wind was cold, stinging and howling way too hard for fly casting. So we split up to take different routes down, agreeing to meet at the outlet of the lowest lake. I came down the feeder creek and caught three small cutthroats right at the inlet. This was only five hundred feet farther down the slope, but that made a lot of difference. It was still cool and breezy, but manageable.

These trout were lying in the open in a clear, slow current and they came up easily to a #16 Adams dry fly. A ptarmigan and Hares Ear soft hackle would have been a more poetic pattern, but that didn't occur to me until days later.

I cleaned the fish, put them in plastic bags and stuffed them into the back of my shooting vest next to my birds. As I headed down through the trees to meet up with Steve and Larry, I started watching the ground. It was a little late in the season, but I thought there might still be a few Boletus mushrooms around (ideal in ptarmigan paprika), and then it occurred to me that between here and the trailhead an enterprising hunter/gatherer could, with a little luck, get into a blue grouse or two and maybe a few brook trout.

Then I saw the error in that and unloaded the shotgun. I've always thought the sight of the interesting but drab birds next to the bright, gorgeous trout implied some subtle comment.

Something like, "The only way you could spoil this for yourself now is by getting greedy."

Sage grouse live at the other end of things, in the sagebrush shrublands variously called the upper Sonoran or high plains desert. Where I've hunted them in northwestern Colorado the terrain comes in swales and gorges separated by flat-topped low hills from the summits of which you can see enormous tracts of land. From vantage points like these you can easily overlook a town of two hundred people unless it's dark and there are lights on.

Sage is the predominant vegetation here, grayish blue, tough, leathery-leaved, rough-barked aromatic stuff (though not the spice you cook with), thicker in the shallow swales, thinner on the low hills. On some of the ridges there will be scattered stands of dark green dwarf junipers. The soil is usually a sandy gray color, poor in quality by farming or grazing standards and littered everywhere with the old bones of cattle, antelope and assorted smaller critters.

It's said that one way to tell the difference between a tree and a shrub is that you can walk under a tree, but you have to walk *around* a shrub. Sage grouse are almost always found near water where the vegetation is thickest, so you walk through—or around, I should say—the thickest sage, salt-bush, greasewood and shadescale, leaving weaving tracks in the powdery soil that resemble those of a drunk.

This is agoraphobic country, the kind that caused the prairie madness in early settlers. Too much exposure to too much great, open space causes certain people to shrink, become transparent and eventually begin to dissolve altogether.

I'm one of those people, but I find that *some* exposure to vastness is cleansing. A couple of days is good. After that I'm longing for the shelter of trees.

Last fall DeWitt Daggett and I were out on the northwestern high plains looking for sage grouse. The procedure here is to drive the endless dirt roads until you find a seep or stock tank—any water at all. Then you hunt the immediate area, flushing the birds if they're there and then moving on.

This is virtually all public land in one way or another, so at dusk you simply pull off to the side of the road and camp. Traffic won't break the mood out here. The nearest town is thirty miles away, and it's a crossroads with a café, gas station and liquor store. The one rule is: Don't roll your sleeping bag out near a fence because antelope jumping over it at night could land on you with their sharp little hooves.

DeWitt and I camped on a low ridge for the view. It was just getting to be dusk by the time we'd gathered enough dead sage for a hot little fire and had the red beans and tortillas going. We'd been out for several days, shooting blue grouse in the Elkhead Mountains and then heading out to the plains to look for some of the big sage grouse, so our camps had become quick and minimal.

DeWitt is a publisher of audiotapes now, but he has a practical science background. In the rambling conversation around the fire the figure of a billion came up somehow, and I confessed that I was now lost. I said, "I can relate to a hundred, a thousand or maybe even ten thousand, but a billion means nothing to me."

DeWitt sprang to his feet and said, "Well, let's see if we can engineer an example."

Using the last of the natural light, we paced off two ten-yard squares, counted the number of sage plants in each one and took an average. I don't remember the actual figures, but it was roughly x number of plants per square yard, then a look at the topo map to figure how many square miles of land we could see from our vantage point.

I stood on the top of the ridge with a can of beer turning slowly round and round to get a feel for this enormous place while DeWitt scribbled the math on a scrap of paper. The sage was like a broken bluish haze from horizon to horizon.

Then DeWitt came up beside me and said, "This is just an informed guess, but I don't think we can see a billion sage plants from here."

I thought I felt my shoes lift off the ground for a second (gravity must have been suspended momentarily as the enormity of that sank in) and then DeWitt said, "I think the beans are done."

I haven't had much experience with sharp-tailed grouse, but I've gone to some lengths to hunt them a few times, if only so I can say I've shot and eaten every grouse species in Colorado and tied trout flies with their feathers.

Sharp-tails live in open grasslands and mountain meadows. This is dry, rolling country with low hills rising away from scrubby stream beds clogged with willow and scrub oak. The meadows are often a uniform golden brown in the fall, with rock ledges at the ridge tops and random outcrops here and there looking like wrecked ships.

As with the other grouse, you can walk a long way looking for a few sharp-tails but, as luck would have it, you can swing along pretty well out there, always watching for mats of cactus and ancient discarded tangles of barbed wire.

The last time I hunted them DeWitt, Larry, Steve, Ed and I spent a day at it and got one bird. We'd been hunting blues in the higher mountains, but there were some huge grassy meadows nearby that were known to hold sharp-tails and we had Dutch the pointer along.

The blues had given Dutch a hard time. The woods were dry—bad for scenting—and the birds were few and far between, which can cause a young pointer to either lose interest or forget what he's doing and begin to think he's just out for a walk.

We drove down from our campsite in the pine woods and walked the meadows. We walked quickly, five abreast, to cover ground, and Dutch bravely busted his little hump to work in front of the whole group.

It must have been five hours before we saw that single grouse. Like a young pointer myself, I had all but forgotten what we were doing. I knew we were walking hard across open, grassy country, getting pretty tired in the process, but feeling well-worked and nice and loose. I guess I was busy experiencing the emptiness: bright blue-and-white sky, wheat-colored grass, cool air. I was carrying the shotgun loosely at my side with very close to nothing on my mind.

I was on the far left end of the line of hunters. When Dutch flushed the grouse, it went straight away, and as I raised the shotgun the bird flared to the left and swung around behind me. It was a fast passing shot over my left shoulder and I must say I dropped the grouse neatly. This was the only sharp-tail I saw that season, and I had inadvertently followed the two best pieces of advice I've ever gotten about wing shooting, namely, "Mount the gun like you mean it" and "Don't think."

This is all fine, but for me it always comes back to blue grouse: my favorite, familiar upland game bird. You find them roughly in the cozy forests that lie between the sprawling, open high plains and the dizzying, open alpine tundra. The grouse that live out where there are no trees to hop up into are more likely to flush (ptarmigan won't always fly, but at least they'll run) and are therefore more stylish.

But I like the forest, so the forest grouse were the first ones that, in my haphazard, unsystematic way, I set out to learn about when I first moved here.

At first it seemed that most Rocky Mountain hunters didn't think much of blue grouse except as a menu item. Almost everyone I talked to admitted to having shot some, but most had done it with big game rifles while hunting deer and elk or with .22 pistols in the interest of camp meat, and they all acted a little sheepish about it. After hearing that story often enough I developed the commonly held opinion that blues *never* fly and that anyone who ever bagged one probably did it in a manner not befitting a gentleman.

The first ones I ever saw—on a hike in springtime—seemed to bear that out by just sitting in a ponderosa pine and looking at me. They were big, handsome birds. If only they hadn't acted like barnyard chickens. The next day I told a friend that I'd seen a couple of fool hens up at the mouth of Skunk Canyon. It's a derisive term, but it does have a certain ring to it when you're trying to fit into a new part of the country.

The first ones I ever shot also just sat there looking at me. I was rabbit hunting, blue grouse season was open, and there were three of them in a pine tree. The daily limit just happens to be three and it's legal to shoot them with all manner of artillery, including the .22 rifle I was carrying. It was all too perfect to resist, and I got two before the third one flushed. Sure enough, you do feel a little sheepish about this, even though everyone does it.

The birds were great roasted, though—all grouse are delicious—and they are great in grouse paprika, boned and stuffed a la Steve Peterson or just about any other way you can think of. I fell into the common misconception that the two best things you could say about blue grouse were that you couldn't actually bludgeon them to death on the ground and that they tasted better than porcupine.

But then I began to hear rumors to the effect that there were, in fact, some hunters around who took these birds seriously. There weren't many of them—a Division of Wildlife biologist told me in the early eighties he thought there might be a few hundred honest blue grouse hunters in the state, tops—but they were mostly guys who carried twenty-gauge doubles and hunted with pointers or Labs. Pointers are said, by the owners of pointers, to be the best because, with their tendency to freeze, blues hold well for a point. The Lab faction says you need a flushing dog, and a big, strong one at that because mountainous blue grouse country can take it out of a dog.

Be that as it may, the word was these grouse hunters mostly shot the birds out of the air, although some did carry .22 pistols, just in case.

That same biologist also told me he couldn't understand

why people didn't hunt blues as avidly as they did sage or sharp-tailed grouse. "They flush as often as not," he said, "and when they do they're as impressive and hard to hit as any game bird."

And they're a big bird. When you first catch sight of one (you're excited and the exact range may not be clear in your mind) you can blow a second or two thinking it's a small wild turkey. And they are *so* good to eat that you won't waste them on just any old dinner guest. A blue grouse is often saved for serious game feasts followed by fine port or a seduction.

By then I had wandered around in the Rocky Mountains long enough to have come upon a number of blues and I had to agree with the biologist that if they stood around like chickens half the time, they flushed thunderously and thrillingly the other half. And, as a second biologist said, "For every dumb one you see in a tree, you probably walked by a dozen smart ones on the ground." That's the number-one reason for using a dog.

The first few times I was properly armed with a shotgun and fired at the flushing birds, I found them to be like geese, that is, a big target that's faster and harder to hit than you think.

I also noticed that they were not all that easy to find. They're often so hard, in fact, that many hunters consider just locating the birds to be the true sport in blue grouse hunting. As a general rule, they like ridge tops, old burns and sometimes the edges of clear cuts. In early fall they're often at lower altitudes in aspen/sage/serviceberry/chokecherry country, although they may have moved uphill by the time the season starts. In practice, they're where you find them, usually near food.

They like conifer needles, the leaves of certain wild shrubs and also the flowers and berries. Sometimes they'll eat bugs, and they're said to have a sweet tooth for grasshoppers.

Blues tend to spend the warmer months at lower altitudes, and then migrate upslope in the winter. During hunting season they are often on the move. In winter they grow feathery snowshoes on their feet so they can get around and have been known to burrow under the snow to stay warm. Through the colder months they exist almost entirely on Douglas fir needles or, in a pinch, those of lodgepole pine. For some reason, they prefer the young needles from older trees.

On the lower end, their range overlaps that of the sage and sharp-tailed grouse. At the higher altitudes, blues are often found near ptarmigan habitat. Bagging all four species in a single trip is a grand slam. It's also a hell of a walk, not to mention a stroke of luck.

For a long time I wondered why they call them "blue" grouse, because the ones I'd seen were all a regulation game bird mottled brownish tan with chocolate, brown and black-marked flank feathers perfect for legs on dark stonefly nymph patterns. But then I saw my first male. He was bigger than the females and he was a dusky bluish gray on the breast: what a fly tier would call a medium blue dun. This stately bird stood proudly on a log about twenty-five yards away, apparently ignoring me, although he'd have flushed if I'd walked up on him. I was hunting snowshoe hares with a small-bore rifle. Grouse season had been over for a couple of weeks.

I think it was inevitable that I would become a genuine blue grouse hunter. At first I just figured that a blue-collar hunter makes the best sport possible out of what's at hand, but these things take on a life of their own. These birds are *grouse*, after all, and I am a grouse *hunter*. Given that, it is impossible to remain casual about it, and if most people wanted to think of them as fool hens, that only made them more endearing.

I learned that blues tend to frequent the same places year after year, based, of course, on food availability and weather patterns. Still, if you see them on a certain ridge in the last week of September one season, there's a good chance they'll be around there next year, too. Like a true blue grouse hunter, I became very closed-mouthed about my few dependable spots.

I learned that it was better to hunt them early in the year when they were still able to feed on berries. That puts them on the ground, and when they're underfoot they often flush beautifully. A diet of berries also gives the meat a luscious, not quite sweet, fruity flavor.

Blues aren't terribly hard to hit when they flush from the ground (a dove or quail hunter will tell you they're a piece of cake), although that's not by any means to say that you can't miss. On a ridge, however, they'll typically swing downhill, presenting a shot that often baffles me. They'll do the same thing coming out of a tree.

The first season I got fairly serious about this, I had a day where four birds flushed from trees, all flying downhill. I shot and missed all four times, and this after putting in three days and many miles uphill and down looking for them. I thought something that still comes to mind ocassionally, but that I haven't said out loud since I was ten years old: "It's too hard, I can't do it, it ain't fair!" Then later, driving home, I thought, these are big, handsome, good-tasting game birds that are hard to find and that you can't always hit. You wanted sport, so quit complaining.

You must do this, too, right? I can't be the only hunter who talks to himself.

So the blue grouse had become a respectable game bird. I stopped calling them fool hens and started thinking about a sweet little twenty-gauge double with an English-style straight stock—the classic English grouse gun. Snazzy shotguns can be more expensive than bamboo fly rods, but the same vision leads you to them: the idea that the tool should be as elegant as the creature it's used to bag. I got the shotgun, and then my old shooting vest started looking seedy. You know how it is.

Now I'd rather kill blue grouse than pheasants or the ruffed grouse I grew up on, nostalgia notwithstanding, or any of the other grouse hereabouts. Everyone has his bird, and this is mine.

And a funny thing has happened over the years: It seems that the more desperately I want them to fly, the more often they do. Maybe the places I thought were my secrets are actually heavily hunted and the birds are spooky, although it's rare for me to run into another grouse hunter. Maybe it's magic. Or maybe they can just smell the adrenaline that's generated by paying a lot of money for a shotgun.

I *do* still find blue grouse sitting in trees from time to time, but I no longer look down on that. These are wild birds and that's just how they are sometimes. I've seen ruffed grouse do the same thing, and I've heard wild tom turkeys gobble back at a car horn. It's just a matter of how you look at it. As I once heard a man say about his country relatives, "They're either ignorant and simple-minded or refreshingly uncomplicated. Take your pick."

When blues are sitting in a tree, the time-honored method of flushing them is to throw sticks at them. This is a skill in itself. When you're alone, lobbing a stick accurately and then getting your shotgun to port arms before the stick hits takes some practice. When you're with a partner, you take turns with the stick. Your friend says, "Ready?" and you say, "Okay, pull!"

Every season does present opportunities to shoot blues out of trees, and it can be a strong temptation, especially after a number of long, grouseless days. The gourmet in you wants the meat, the fly tier wants the feathers and the sportsman wants to take the game in a skillful, honorable way. It's a quandary, but it's probably useful to be presented with a value judgment that you must make fresh each time. It's a kind of ethical calisthenics.

Some hunters turn the old survival rule around. "Shoot the top one first," they say. "When he falls, he might flush the rest." The one thing you can be sure of is, when you show up with a limit of blues someone will say, "Shot 'em out of a tree, huh?" and you really want to be able to say, "Nope. On the wing. All of 'em."

This can become the kind of technical point that requires a finely honed sense of sporting ethics to appreciate. A few years ago a friend and I had a single bird sitting in a tree—the classic fool hen situation. Taking turns, we had each thrown several dozen sticks and rocks at the thing, but the most he'd do was duck. We were getting a little fed up with this, and my friend's poor springer spaniel was going nuts.

Finally, when it was my turn with the gun, my partner clipped the grouse with what would have been a good piece of campfire wood, and the bird hopped from one limb to another, at which point I harvested him, as they say.

"At least you shot him off a different branch," my friend said.

"Branch, hell," I said. "That bird was in the air."

4

Bugs

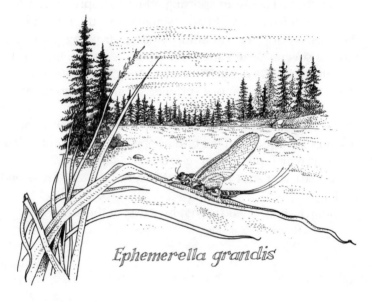

Ephemerella grandis

Some years ago I was fishing the Green Drake mayfly hatch on Idaho's Henry's Fork with a couple of friends; it was the first time I'd ever attended one of these famous hatches on what people still insist on calling a "world-class fishery."

Well, maybe that's not entirely true. Back home in Colorado I'd fished hatches that had been written about in books and magazines on rivers people might have heard of, but your local water is different somehow. You don't have to buy a nonresident license and half the time you end up back in your own bed the same night, which makes it all seem strangely ordinary.

I guess it's just that I'd heard a lot about the Green Drake hatch on the Henry's Fork, but I'd never driven all the way up there to see it and, since this was known as a place where the really serious fishermen went, the trip felt a little like a pilgrimage.

The first day we stopped in at Mike Lawson's fly shop and I overheard a guide referring to this event as the "Gortex hatch," an allusion to all the spiffy fly fishers in town, half of whom looked like models from one of the more expensive catalogs. (The guide didn't mind that my friends and I were standing right there because we clearly didn't fit into the snappy sportsman category.)

Some of these guys had come from faraway places like Pennsylvania and New York, and they were not only well-dressed, they also seemed to be awfully knowledgeable about this and other hatches. There was a subtle academic atmosphere in and around Last Chance, Idaho. Over breakfast at the café you'd hear as much Latin as you would English.

It was a little intimidating, but if I didn't exactly fit in here, I felt I could at least hold my own in a pinch. I knew, for instance, that the Green Drake mayfly in question was the *Ephemerella grandis*—not to be confused with the almost identical *E. doddsi* or the similar but smaller *E. flavilinea.*

I'd done some homework on this hatch because I understood that bugs are the key to fly-fishing. Or, to be more correct, you might say "insects." Then again, allowing that a trout's diet could include some critters that are not technically in the class Insecta (like scuds and such), maybe you'd want to say "food organisms." This is how it begins: You start to get a burr under your saddle about accuracy.

We'd tied some flies for the trip—standard, by-the-book drake patterns with collar hackles and split wings—but that year everyone on the Fork was using the newer, fancier Paradrake, the one with the bullet-headed deer hair body, parachute hackle and extended abdomen. So we bought some of those for what, at the time, was the most I'd ever paid for store-bought flies.

The first thing I did when I got on the water was to whip

out my ten-cent aquarium net and catch one of the fabled *Ephemerellas* because that's what a properly scientific fly fisher does, especially when there are other fishermen watching. It was a pretty bug all right; beautiful, in fact. At first glance it's just a large, grayish-green mayfly, but then you notice that the soft-looking underside of the abdomen is a pale olive, while the back is hard and gray, with fine green lines between the segments. The shell-like, gray armor extends up the back in overlapping plates to the head. The tibia of the legs are pale green, but the femurs are an iron gray. The wings are slate-colored and darkly veined, but there's a small green patch at the base of each costal margin.

Not knowing what else to do with it, I compared the bug to the Para-drake. Considering that no trout fly exactly copies the real creature, this imitation looked okay (maybe a little too fat and too green), but out on the current when the drift was right it looked great: I think "perky" was the accepted term.

I'll admit that there was a certain feeling of power in knowing the Latin name for the bugs on the water. Never mind that I knew only because I'd been told by people who *really* knew, there was still this vague sense of mastery.

But then there's always someone around who doesn't seem to care about any of that and who's happily catching fish anyway, which is puzzling as hell to the novice entomologist. That week on the Henry's Fork I kept running into this old guy dressed in coveralls and a T-shirt. He was catching a lot more trout than I was, so I finally waded over and asked him what he was using.

"Green fly," he said. "These bugs are green, so you gotta have a green fly."

Right. That's pretty much what the fishermen back at the café were saying, only he said it in English.

My friends and I stayed there for most of a week, and we all caught trout. On the days when the sky was that bright, pure western blue, the hatch was thin and didn't last too long. On the gray, low-ceiling days, the flies poured off the river by the thousands from nine in the morning until midafternoon. We did well overall, and during the best parts of the best days the fish were almost easy to catch.

Between the peak times for the Green Drakes there were usually some *Ephemerella infrequens* or *inermis* (large and small Pale Morning Duns) on the water, and we spent a couple of nights downstream fishing to an *Ephemera simulans* (Brown Drake) hatch. We bought Green and Brown Drake flies at Lawson's (same pattern, different size and color) and we used our own Pale Morning Duns because those little Henry's Fork bugs were pretty much like the ones we had back home.

We did try to use the scientific names for a while, but we soon slipped back into the comfortable—and traditional— procedure of calling the bugs by the names of the flies used to imitate them. I don't know about the others, but I began to think that the Latin sounded a little hollow coming from me because I didn't really know what I was talking about. That first morning when I marched into the fly shop and asked what fly pattern was producing the best on the *Ephemerella grandis* hatch, it was just a pretentious way of saying, "Gimme a dozen of whatever's workin'."

I will say that knowing about the bugs can be extremely helpful at times. There's some real hard-nosed fishing stuff there that will sometimes cause you to catch trout when you otherwise wouldn't, or catch more of them when you'd only have caught a few.

Understanding just the basic lifecycles and typical behavior of the various bugs—which is both the first and last step for many of us—will tell you that if mayflies, caddis flies or midges are hatching, there are emerging nymphs or pupae just beneath them under the surface, but that when it's stoneflies, mating caddis or mayfly spinners on the water, there are no hidden emergers.

Or let's say there's a mayfly hatching and the trout aren't

taking the fly pattern that seems to imitate the dun. If you know what the bug is, you'll know what that particular emerging nymph looks like, what color it is and how it acts, which means you won't have to guess which nymph pattern to tie on or how to fish it.

If it's one of the *Ephemerellas* known as Green Drakes, you'll even know that the bug usually sheds its nymphal husk deep in the water and swims to the surface as a winged fly, so the floating nymph pattern you'd use for another mayfly probably won't work. What works is something that looks a lot like an old-style wet fly, only bigger and greener than most.

If you know beforehand that the hatch is an *Ephemera simulans* mayfly, you'll not only buy or tie up Brown Drake dry flies, you'll also know that the hatch will probably be in the evening, that there's a simultaneous spinner fall that you had better have flies for and that the nymphs have prominent gills. You may want to painstakingly tie individual feather tip gills on the abdomens of all your nymphs or just tease out the dubbing on a Hares Ear pattern with your pocketknife. Your response is a matter of personal style. The point is, you know something useful.

If you do much fly-fishing you'll eventually absorb a cursory knowledge of the bugs just from listening to people and reading the odd book, but in my experience genuine angling entomologists are few and far between, and those who haven't written a book are extremely rare. The precious few I've met seem to fit a certain profile. They probably started out doing what I still do, that is, getting the species designation from someone at the local fly shop and then looking up some particulars in one of the bug books, maybe learning something helpful in the process. At first they did that just to get a leg up on the hatch and catch more trout, and, like most of us with a little knowledge, they were at least tempted to drop enough terminology into their conversations to impress their buddies.

But eventually they became honestly fascinated by the

loveliness and complexity of what happens on trout streams and began to engage in some real study and observation. That might have cut into their fishing time a little at first, but they didn't care about that because they'd been grabbed by a healthy curiosity about the environments where they spend so much time. If their accumulated knowledge finally gave them an advantage over the trout, they accepted that fact with some grace and used it, but their real advantage is over other fishermen. An authentic entomologist can have as much fun looking at bugs as you or I have catching fish.

And if the hatch of the moment is a size eighteen Blue Quill Dun, then that's how they'll describe it. They won't look you in the eye and call it a *Baetis spinosus* sudimago by way of a gut check.

I kept studying bugs for a while because that's what one did if one wanted to become serious about fly-fishing—and seriousness, in a sort of Zen sense, is what we all secretly aspire to—but I also kept running into these archetypal old guys who were catching lots of big fish on the apparently simple-minded premise that if the bugs on the water were, say, small and dark, you had to use a small, dark fly. One of them even told me, pointedly, that learning more about bugs than the trout know is a waste of time.

So I never became a real angling entomologist. For one thing, I have reservations about science as the One True Way to understand reality. Luckily, there are other good vantage points. If there weren't, many of us would have to go through life hopelessly ignorant. I remember this exchange from a PBS science program:

Earnest interviewer: "Can you put that in layman's terms?"

Rumpled physicist: "No."

To put it another way, an ichthyologist knows about trout and an entomologist knows about bugs, but it's the fly tier who knows how to fool a trout into thinking something is a bug when it's not.

I decided I was more comfortable with fly-fishing as a folk art rather than a science and, to be honest, I realized I wanted to know about bugs for the wrong reasons. That is, it was really enough for me that the bugs were there, the trout ate them and there were fly patterns that imitated them. As for the rest, I guess I just suffered for a while under the delusion that you can somehow bludgeon trout into submission if you just have enough facts, and if that doesn't work you can at least intimidate other fishermen.

Maybe this reveals a deep character flaw (other fishermen get good at this without turning into creeps) or maybe it is just a stage you go through on the way to deciding what kind of outdoorsman you're going to be. Whatever, during my short entomological phase, I saw that I was like the guy who takes up the guitar not because he loves music, but because he thinks it will attract women.

I do own five books on trout stream insects, and I've actually read two of them—the last one, published in 1975, was drier and more detailed than the first, which was published in 1955. Now and then, if someone who actually knows can tell me the species of bug that might be hatching, I'll look it up to see about recommended patterns, hatch times and fishing tactics, but I usually don't care that the nymph has eight posterio-lateral spines on the abdomen or that the median vein on the hind wing of the dun is distinctly forked at slightly less than halfway to its base. Maybe I should care, but I just don't.

If I now toss around terms like *Baetis* or *Trike* (short for *Tricorythodes*) it's only because that stuff is common knowledge, and on those trips where I slip and begin dropping what to me are largely useless, often inaccurate bits of taxonomy, one of my friends usually shuts me down.

Once, on a drive through Montana, a friend and I stopped for gas. It was nighttime, and the lighted gas pumps were covered with mayflies from a nearby trout stream. I said, "Hey, look at this!"

My partner—a notorious deflater of egos—peered at the

bugs and said, "Yeah, *Parallelia flavahoovias,* right?"

That's a point. If you were a consummate phony with an ear for dead languages, you could make this stuff up and sound pretty good to a gullible greenhorn. And I guess I *had* been spouting a little amateur entomology.

For all practical purposes, the flies were Red Quill spinners, about a size sixteen. Whatever species of mayfly they represented, we knew they'd be forming up into a mating flight over the riffles in the evenings and that the trout would feed on them in the first slower water downstream. We could also safely figure that riffles near the gas station would be a good bet.

We were on our way somewhere else to catch other trout, but if we'd stayed there until the next evening we'd have known what to do, and that was comforting.

5

Texas

DAHLBERG DIVER

GUADALUPE BASS

*T*he Texas hill country north of San Antonio struck me as wildly foreign and strangely familiar at the same time. The rolling topography forested in live oak, pin oak, walnut, pecan and such reminded me of the Midwest where I was born, as did the humidity and the small, old towns built around shady courthouse squares, but of course there are differences. Try to picture rural Ohio but with armadillos, ringtails, rattlesnakes, cactus, great Mexican food and hard-scrabble goat ranches instead of farms.

And then there's *poco tiempo*: the slow pace, of which Texan English is one example. It's a lovely language to hear spoken, and after a few days of it you come to realize that you'd drawl too if you had plenty of time to speak your piece and could assume your listeners were too polite to interrupt. Pause to search for the right word, and everyone waits patiently. It's amazing. You find yourself saying pretty much what you meant to say instead of just blurting something out.

Ed Engle and I drove down there in April to do some "real" bass fishing, as opposed to whatever kind of bass fishing it is we do back home in Colorado. The possibility of bigger fish was part of it, but more than that we wanted to catch bass in a place where they belong—as opposed to a place like Colorado where they've been introduced—in the company of people who grew up there and really know how to do it.

This is important because to catch a certain kind of fish you must come to understand them, and that understanding becomes part of the character of a place. That's why fishermen are almost as interesting as the fish themselves.

We were in Ed's old Datsun pickup with my new Mansfield canoe strapped on top. This truck doesn't have a proper boat rack on it, so we had jury-rigged one with foam blocks and lots of rope. If we hadn't had to stop to retie the canoe every hundred miles or so, we might have cut a few hours off the trip. As it was, it took the better part of two days.

Ed and I aren't kids anymore, but we still believe in the hip romance of long road trips—you know, the boredom, risk, sense of purpose and the distance from all that stuff that, before you left, seemed too damned important.

The first night we slept in a park somewhere near Big Spring, Texas. We'd spent an hour in town asking people where we could camp and no one seemed to know what we were talking about.

"You mean park a camper?"

"No, we mean 'camp,' you know, sleep on the ground."

We were a little road-burned and I suggested getting a room, which we both usually consider to be the same as giving up, or at least giving in to lazy, middle-class comfort. But Ed held out for a quick, cheap camp. Our road trips have always been low-budget by necessity, and at this stage of the game a room just seems like a needless extravagance. And, as Ed the pragmatist says, "You should always scrimp early on a trip because you never know what you'll run into later."

Finally a woman at a gas station said it would be all right if we slept in the park just down the road. It wasn't clear whether it was all right officially or just all right with her, but it was dark, we were tired and we didn't pursue it.

It took about ten minutes to toss out the sleeping bags and set up the camp stove. Then I started supper while Ed drove back into town to call home. Seems his wife, Monica, was having some trouble at work serious enough that she might lose the job. Ed had offered to cancel the trip so he could be there during the crisis, but Monica had said, no, go, staying won't make any difference. Bless her heart. I've always liked Monica.

I was sitting at a picnic table under a street light surrounded by a thousand bugs, drinking a Lone Star beer and trying to keep at least the larger insects out of the stew. I've made some of those calls myself—the ones where you feel like you really should be home, even though you probably couldn't be much help, but instead you're on a trip, supposedly having fun, although you're not having as much fun as you might ordinarily because you really should be home. You feel slightly irresponsible, but you know in your heart that life is short and responsibility is overrated.

I could picture it: Ed calling home from an outside pay phone to see about the trouble, the trucks on the highway drowning out parts of the conversation. First she'd ask, "Where are you calling from?" and Ed would say, "Big Spring." That probably wouldn't mean anything, but she'd try to picture it anyway. Was it a nice little town or a neon shithole along the highway?

All the calls I've made like that seemed crucial at the time, although now I can't remember what a single one of them was about. All I remember is the feeling. It's not loneliness; more like just the experience of distance.

Ed was back in fifteen minutes. He got a beer from the cooler and said, "It's okay, at least for the time being. *Now* I'm glad I came." That's about as specific as Ed ever gets about things like this. He's a bit of a cynic (he once told me his only retirement plan was to have a massive heart attack) but he's not a whiner, so it's: "Well, there's a little trouble, but when isn't there?" and then some time later, "Oh, that. I guess it turned out okay."

It's not that Ed won't bitch if you get him started, but about personal matters he exhibits a kind of restraint I've always admired: a sort of things-are-a-mess-but-I'm-okay attitude that makes him more likely to argue than complain.

We made Mason, Texas, by late afternoon the next day, and checked into the motel where we were supposed to meet our unofficial guides, Bud Priddy and Joe Robinson. The drive seemed to go quickly. The conversation was more spirited because we were getting closer to actually going fishing and because Ed had a load off his mind. And then there was a lift, literally and figuratively, as we drove up out of the scrubby plains into the forested hills around Mason County.

Bud showed up in time for supper—burritos at a little café on the corner—and Joe arrived some time after dark. It was a hot night, so we sat in the air-conditioned room to discuss our strategy. The first order of business was to float the Llano River in canoes for two days, camping overnight on an island. That's permissible. "Islands are considered no man's land," Bud said.

Ed and I were concerned about what was permissible because there is almost no public land or water in Texas. Everything is so uniformly private—and trespassing is so universally frowned upon—that most land isn't even posted. The assumption is that you will exhibit the proper respect, and if you don't you'll learn damned quick and in no uncertain terms. This made us a little nervous, coming from

Colorado where there's more public than private land to wander around on.

So in our midwestern Germanic way, Ed and I wanted to know the rules. Bud said, "Well, there's things that'll get you yelled at and things that won't." Joe added, "It's best not to go acting like a hippie *in front of people.*"

Officially, you can put your canoe in and take it out at road crossings on navigable rivers. In between, you'll probably be okay if you conduct yourself like a gentleman. You'll naturally get out of the canoe from time to time to wade, cast from the bank, have lunch and relieve yourself, and all of that *may* be illegal. If you want to do this yourself, don't just bring a copy of this book. Contact the State of Texas Parks and Wildlife Department.

These lush, pretty, spring-fed hill country rivers are perfect for a canoe paddled by people who are less than experts: mostly slow flowing and lazy, but with enough rocks and rapids to make things interesting. Ed and I were using my new Mansfield canoe, a sweet little boat with thin cedar strut construction inside and an equally thin fiberglass shell. It's pretty and delicate looking, and when we lifted it off the top of the truck Joe said, "Nice boat. I hope you don't bust it up in here."

I thought he was giving us some of that good-natured grief, but when I looked at his eyes I realized he was honestly wishing us well. He really hoped we wouldn't bust it up.

These streams are not only pretty, they're also rich in fish: several species of sunfish (called "perch" locally), catfish big enough for head mounts, carp, alligator gar and some largemouth bass, but the definitive fish is the Guadalupe bass. These are small, stream-dwelling bass native only to a few rivers in Texas.

Guadalupe bass are somewhat troutlike in their habits, even to their tendency to feed daintily on mayflies below riffles, and local fly fishermen like to call them "Texas brook trout." They even look a little like trout in the water. The coloration varies, but many Guadalupe bass have distinct spots and bronzish-green backs; actually more like a cutthroat than a brookie.

The only catch is that they seldom grow to more than two pounds, so many bass fishermen overlook them and, as near as I can tell, the trout fishermen who would appreciate them don't usually *go* to Texas.

Fly-fishing is considered a minor angling method in Texas, and fly-fishing for small stream fish with light tackle is a downright rarefied sport. Before this was over we'd spend four days on rivers, and in that time we'd see one other boat, from which no one was fishing.

So there was that cockeyed familiarity again. The Llano was wider and slower than most Rocky Mountain streams, but there were rock cliffs and it was flowing water with bright, spotted fish, and so completely recognizable. But then when you got out to wade and fish you didn't need waders because the water was warm, and you usually fished something like a deer hair frog instead of a mayfly—although you *could* fish a mayfly during a hatch and do well.

The banks were forested with deciduous trees filled with cardinals and, unless you count the odd trotline set for catfish, there were no signs of civilization. If I wasn't casting a little cork or deer hair froggie along the banks and picking up fish, I was paddling with long, slow strokes trying to keep Ed in the best casting position. If you're fond of canoes, one is about as much fun as the other. The newness of the place sank in quickly and I became pretty happy.

We took turns paddling and fishing and tried to look around as much as possible, knowing that you'll never see enough of a new river in just a couple of days. I saw a snake that could have been a cottonmouth and a mature white-tailed deer no bigger than a Great Dane. The deer are tiny here, stunted because there are so many of them.

We each caught our first Guadalupe bass, first yellow-bellied perch, first long ear. You couldn't tell what kind of fish you had by the strike, but once hooked the largemouth bass would often jump, Guadalupe bass would jump higher and the panfish would plane heavily with their flat sides against the current.

Sometimes we'd beach the canoe to admire and photograph these fish, and then there'd be a strange bird we had to get a look at. I saw a little green kingfisher: another first.

Often the two canoes were far apart, but sometimes you'd catch bits of conversation. Once, after an hour of virtual silence, I heard a thump and Joe's slow voice saying, "Bud, I believe that bass just took a bite out of your boat."

The first night we camped on an island of bleached round river stones that would not take a tent peg. Bud cooked steaks and beans and made biscuits in a Dutch oven while Ed and I went through the guidebook trying to identify, from memory, some of the unfamiliar birds we'd seen. We turned the canoes over to drain. Mine had taken a few scratches, but we hadn't busted it up.

The island is accessible by car over a narrow bridge, and just as we were all crawling into our tents a pickup with two young couples pulled in. They saw our camp, talked it over for a minute and left. In the polite way Texans have, Joe suggested that they'd driven out there to "look at the moon" and required a little more privacy.

A few days later we were in south Texas looking for the entrance to a private fishing camp. In between there had been a party at a Mexican restaurant in San Antonio with great food, lots of beer, many wild fishing stories and an awful mariachi band. I'm as multicultural as the next guy, but I draw the line at mariachi bands with no sense of rhythm and two flat trumpets. One of the guys at our table went over and tipped the band leader. When he came back I asked, "You like that?" and he said, "Hell no, that's how you make them go away."

Joe had gone home and we'd picked up a man named

Tommy and his huge, apparently oceangoing, metal flake red bass boat with white Naugahyde swivel seats and chrome steering wheel. There were no dingleberries only because there was no place to hang them. This thing was towed, at great speed, by one of those enormous pickups with the four wheels in back.

The camp consisted of one big building—which was mostly kitchen—that you might call the main lodge, surrounded by several trailers, outbuildings and a collection of possibly abandoned trucks. There was a small airstrip off to the side with a limp orange wind sock hanging from a pole and cracks in the paving through which weeds were growing. As we pulled up, a flock of maybe twenty wild turkeys darted off into the mesquite and cactus.

People in Texas sometimes use a kind of enviable economy in their conversation. Bud could have warned me specifically about rattlesnakes, water moccasins, scorpions, poisonous spiders, wild boars, cats claw bushes, killer bees and such, but instead he just said, as we were getting out of the car, "Now, be careful. Everything down here will either sting you or bite you."

Ed now refers to that first afternoon as the Comanche Tank Disaster. (There are no bass ponds in Texas, but there are plenty of "tanks.") While Bud and I were getting the aluminum john boat into the water, Tommy backed his trailer way too far and too fast out into the tank and got both the trailer and the truck stuck in the deep, clinging mud.

Bud told me to get into the john boat, cranked up the outboard and said he thought the fishing would be best way over there on the other side of the six-hundred-acre lake. As we pulled away, Tommy was gunning the pickup. You could see the rear wheels sinking deeply into the mud, the dual exhausts blowing big bubbles in the muddy water.

I got most of the rest of it secondhand from Ed. Tommy fought the truck and trailer until they were both stuck up to the axles, but the trailer still wasn't deep enough to float the bass boat and it was too heavy to push off. Tommy tried, and he might have done it. He was about seven feet tall, weighed several hundred pounds, and looked strong, but that was offset by many old injuries from a few seasons of playing professional football, as well as numerous other accidents before and since.

Once Tommy was out deer hunting at this very camp. He was riding a dirt bike with a scoped .270 slung over his shoulder when he spotted a big rattlesnake and decided to run over it. (Rattlers are killed on sight in Texas.) But the snake got caught in the front tire, flipped up into Tommy's lap and the whole assembly—bike, snake, rifle and rider—did half a dozen forward somersaults. Tommy was unhappy about that because he "busted the damn gun."

Ed suggested calling a wrecker to pull the truck out of the tank (there was a phone in the pickup), but Tommy said, "They'd never find us out here," which seemed true enough.

Sometime during the struggle Ed's graphite rod got broken, he lost track of his Hardy reel, and then Tommy called someone on the car phone, said, "Hi. Oh, we're stuck in the lake, what're you up to?" and chatted for half an hour.

Then they decided to walk back to the camp for help, took a short cut and got lost.

Bud and I had a nice time catching some bass and watching the pelicans. Later, when Ed accused me of abandoning him, I thought of several excuses, but finally just said, "You're right, I'm sorry."

Then Ed said, in an admiring tone, "You've always been good at sidestepping the weird shit."

Over the next few days we fished the big Comanche Tank and several smaller ones where fly-fishing was a little more reasonable, places like the Frog Tank, Rock Tank and a few others the names of which I either didn't catch or wasn't told. We were in the company of half a dozen middle-aged men who, apparently, had all played high-school football together. Football is a big deal in Texas. You can drive through many small towns without learning their names, but you'll by God know they're the home of the Cougars or the Trojans or whatever.

One of these guys took us aside and said that, although Tommy seemed big and dangerous, he was really just accident prone, but otherwise gentle as a lamb. "Just give him plenty of room," the man said.

The standard tactic in these tanks was to fish a floating bug with the diving fly routine. You start by cutting off half of the sinking portion of a sink-tip fly line and throwing it away. Then, on the part that's left, you tie on a short, stout leader— maybe four feet of fifteen- or twenty-pound monofilament— and attach a bass bug to the business end with a Duncan Loop, a knot that lets the fly wiggle around, even on a stiff leader.

Bud's flies of choice are Dahlberg Diver–style deer hair bugs. The standard froggie is good, but Bud also has some patterns of his own design, including an injured baitfish and a neat little baby catfish with rubber whiskers. Bud ties some of the best-looking deer hair bugs I've ever seen. They're right up there with the ones tied by Dave Whitlock and Jimmy Nix: trim but buggy, tails perfectly matched, deer hair spun tight as cork.

Anyway, you cast the bug up against the bank, a weed bed or flooded stump. When the sinking tip of the line has bellied out under the surface of the water, you give it a good pull and the floating deer hair bug dives with a beautiful wiggling, swimming motion, kicking its feather legs behind it. I tried other flies, but it only works right with a Dahlberg Diver. I don't know how Larry Dahlberg figured this out, but it was a stroke of genius.

Sometimes the bass do hit like outdoor writers say they do—"like a freight train" is what you usually hear—but more often the take is so subtle you can think the fly has just bumped a weed or a waterlogged stick. Consequently, you set up on everything, and you set up hard, pulling line with your left hand and raising the rod tip with your right. "The harder the better," Bud said. "You want to cross his eyes."

We caught a lot of what I think of as big largemouth bass, but of course the locals outfished us, which is only right and proper. Most of these guys were Ugly Stick and rubber worm fishers, and they were good. Some of them, when they saw that Bud, Ed and I were fly-fishing, dug into their incredible piles of gear, got out their own fly rods, to be polite, and outfished us *that* way.

The often-written-about style of bass bugging, where you fish a floating deer hair bug on a floating line, letting it sit perfectly still on the surface for two, three minutes between gentle twitches, is not much thought of here. "That was invented by some goddamn outdoor writer from up north," Bud said. "These fish are aggressive and you gotta go after 'em aggressively."

He seemed to be right about that, but then this was the way I knew to fish for bass, and in a tank that was so choked with weeds they said it would be unfishable in another couple of weeks, I tried it. I cast a big Near Enough deer hair froggie to the edge of a five-foot-wide pothole of open water, let it sit there for two, three, maybe four minutes and then gave it a twitch.

The fly went down in a rise that looked like a toilet flushing. That's what bass fishers say. It's not the prettiest analogy in angling, but, I'm sorry, that's exactly what it looks like.

I was fishing a stiff, nine-foot, nine-weight rod and had already learned that if you gave a fish even a foot or two of line in these overgrown tanks you'd lose him in the weeds. So the fights were short and brutal. You'd grab the rod in both hands and haul, figuring you had spare rods back in the car, so you could break one, which would at least make for a good story. The bass would either throw the hook or come to the apron of the belly boat still thrashing. That day I got a case of tendonitis in my right elbow that lasted most of the season.

I think that bass weighed eight pounds, so figure seven. I held it up for Bud at a distance and he later said, "Now that was a *big* ol' bass." He was probably being kind. Usually the technical term "big ol' bass" refers to something in the ten-pound class.

That was the prettiest of all the tanks we fished. It was set in flat mesquite country with an enormous horizon and was full of tough weeds, bleached flooded timber and water moccasins they said you should watch out for because they like to crawl up on your belly boat. There were big white-winged whistling ducks that made an eerie, piping call that sounded like the first few notes of a sad folk song. Tommy said that if you got up on the dam and looked west over the tops of the mesquite bushes you could see Mexico. "And if you see dark-haired people running through the bushes," he added, "don't wave."

That night we ate home-cooked tacos at another camp that seemed abandoned, except that the electricity was still on. It was just dark and a storm was coming in from the southwest, so we stood at the open door for a while and watched the lightning. A guy who had made a comment about animal rights nuts two days ago picked up a gallon tub of guacamole dip and said, "Just think how many guacamoles had to die to make this."

The conversations in these fishing camps had less to do with fishing than I'm used to. These men were there to catch bass, but it was generally known where the fish were and how to catch them, so there just didn't seem to be a lot to discuss. Instead there was a lot of catching up. Those who hadn't played football together were distantly related or had once worked for or worked with or been the neighbor of a cousin or great-uncle or had shot deer on the same ranch as boys or *something.* When two strangers meet in Texas they pick each other's pasts apart until they find that connection, a whole universe of discourse opens up, and then they're buddies, if not actual relatives.

Once that's done, conversations take place in which little

is apparently said. One night the name of a girl everyone had known in high school came up. A quiet smile went around the room that I thought I recognized as the prelude to an off-color story, but instead someone said, "Well, she was a pretty girl and she's grown into a handsome married woman." Everyone agreed. "Yes sir, a *hand*some married woman."

One of the best parts of this leg of the trip was all the fish we ate. These tanks are extremely rich in food organisms and the climate is such that bass will spawn several times in a season, so the prevailing management philosophy is that they need to be harvested heavily so they won't overpopulate. "Now kill all the little bass you catch," they kept saying.

"What's 'little'?" I'd ask.

"Oh, say five pounds."

"Back home we'd think about *mounting* a five-pound bass," I said.

"Yeah, I know."

Tommy turned out to be the best cook. He didn't exactly teach me how to make mustard beer battered fish—when I asked him how he did it after the fact he said he couldn't remember—but I watched him do it a few times and picked it up. You mix equal parts mustard and yellow cornmeal, add a dash of baking powder and maybe some hickory salt or whatever else is lying around in the spice department and enough beer to make a thin paste. Then batter the fish and deep fry them in hot Crisco until they're just brown. And watch out for the spitting grease.

I never did land the ten-pound bass on a fly rod—which you can do in south Texas—but I had one on. At least that's what a gentleman named Dan said from the seat next to me in the big red bass boat one day. I was fishing some kind of streamer on a sink-tip line and had gotten a little lazy, as you can do on a hot day, fishing from a plush seat, roll casting with your right hand and holding a cold Lone Star in your left.

The fish hit, I struck and had him on for about as long as it took for him to come to the surface, jump and throw the hook. "That would have gone about ten," Dan said casually. "You shoulda set up harder."

I was trying to fix in my mind that fleeting glimpse of the biggest largemouth bass I'd ever seen alive and I almost said, "How the hell am I supposed to set up harder with a beer in my hand?" but of course the answer was obvious. You *can* fish and drink at the same time, but you can't do both well.

Later I told Ed about the big bass that had gotten off. He said, "Well, that's another one you can think about for the rest of your life."

A day or two later, Bud, Ed and I were back in the hill country, staying at a campground on the Nueces (pronounced "new aces") River. We were a few miles from Camp Wood, the little town where Bud, who now lives in San Antonio, was born. Ed and I were beginning to show signs that the trip was winding down—wondering what was happening at home, talking about work. If we'd stuck to the original plan, we'd have been in northern New Mexico by then, but this was one of those trips that takes on a life of its own. When Bud suggested canoeing one more river, we'd gotten a second wind and called home to say we'd be a little late.

Ed said, "Well, one of us is still employed," meaning Monica. Ed makes a living as a writer and fishing guide, but he wisely doesn't think of either as "employment."

We were a man short for the float the next day—you need a fisherman *and* a paddler per canoe—so we spent a few hours locating Bud's friend Don who, Bud said, "needed to go fishing." Don was a tall, wiry man with a handlebar mustache and one of those silver belt buckles the size of a saucer. He had apparently done many things in life, judging by his stories, but was now happy to be an ostrich rancher. He told us about ostriches in some detail in camp that night, as huge Hexagenia mayflies from the river collected on the picnic table and flying beetles the size of golf balls buzzed the lantern.

The Llano River had been clear, as someone said, "In that pea green way those warm rivers have," but the Nueces was as limpid as any trout stream I've ever seen. Glancing over the gunnels of the canoe in a deep hole, you could count the scales on a bluegill at ten feet.

Bud said the river was fishing a little slow. The water did seem a bit cool and, as clear as it was, it was running a little high. The weather had been chilly for spring in Texas—in the eighties—and there'd been a couple of horrendous rains. In fact, we'd talked about floating the Guadalupe River, but it was blown out by high water.

The Nueces *was* slow in the morning, but it was a bright, almost hot day and by noon the water had warmed and we started getting into fish. Sometimes we'd stop and wade, but more often we'd drift along a shady bank with one man paddling and the other casting. The river was slow enough in most places that if you hit a good bank you could paddle back upstream and drift down again.

We portaged around a few rapids on the Nueces, but I had already put some scratches on my no-longer-new canoe on the Llano, so I had gotten a little braver by then.

Maybe the fishing *was* a little slow, but then Bud has fished these rivers off and on all his life, so he has a different perspective. You have to understand that when a local fisherman tells you how a river usually is, he's describing the best day anyone ever had there. It seemed fine to me and, it being toward the end of the trip and all, I'd have been happy enough just to float and look around, experiencing that edgy sadness you feel when it's almost over, but you still have a hard, two-day drive ahead of you. We did catch fish, but I considered them a bonus.

I guess I had finally achieved the regional pace. I didn't really notice that until I got back home, decompressed for a day, and then forged ahead at what I thought was my normal speed, which is none too fast anyway. Down at the café someone asked, "Are you still tired from your trip?" and I said, "Why, no, darlin', I'm just relaxed," remembering too late that "darlin'" is politically incorrect in Colorado.

I also found that I wasn't bragging. When asked if I got into fish, I allowed as how some folks had been nice enough to show me how to do it and, yes, I did catch a few.

For a couple of days there I was even hesitant to criticize people, tending to say either nice things or nothing at all, as in, "Oh, I don't think he's incompetent, he's probably just in the wrong line of work." It wore off eventually, but for a week or so I was actually acting like a gentleman.

CHAPTER

6

The Curse

A.K. and I have been fishing together for I don't know how long now, and early on in our loose partnership a seemingly odd karmic undertone began to make itself known: For some reason, when one of us does well, the other does poorly, or at least not *as* well.

If one of us catches lots of fish, the other catches only a few or, rarely, none. If A.K. gets into big fish one day, I typically get into the little ones. If we're fishing a warm water pond, one of us will catch only bluegills and pumpkinseeds while the other will get all the bass. It doesn't exactly alternate from day to day, but it does seem to even out over time.

Of course it doesn't always happen that way, which makes

it seem even stranger. There have been a few notable times when we both caught lots of big fish or both got completely skunked, but those days seemed weird, and were only exceptions that proved the rule.

We don't talk about this much anymore, but when we do, we refer to it as The Curse.

For a while I thought it was just us. Years ago we decided not to compete with each other on the stream. This wasn't something we had to hash out; it just happened, we noticed it, and agreed it was for the best. After all, most competition isn't about what it *appears* to be about, and two people bickering about who's the better fisherman are often getting at something much deeper and nastier than that.

So, since neither one of us had an ax to grind, we became friends, but I think the normal parrying and testing still goes on at another, more subtle level, and I once thought The Curse was some kind of spooky subconscious thing caused by suppressed male aggressiveness—or whatever the latest New Age term is for macho.

But then I started hearing the same kind of stories about other fishing partnerships, and some of these guys were real fish-counters, so they had the actual figures to back up their claims. They didn't usually get dramatic about it, they just said things like, "We were fishing the same hatch with the same flies, but it was definitely Mike's day. Seems like that happens a lot—one way or the other."

Eventually, to make life easier, I filed this under the growing category of interesting but inexplicable phenomena or "things for which even elegant explanations are meaningless." I started this file way back in college when I met a philosophy student who made a good case that buses didn't really exist, but still wouldn't step in front of one on a ten-dollar bet.

Early last spring, A.K. and I went down to the South Platte River near the town of Deckers, Colorado, to see about the

Blue-winged Olive hatch. It was a little bit early, but we'd heard that the mayflies were a week or two ahead of schedule and figured it was worth a try. We watched the weather reports for a few days waiting for one of those gray, gloomy days when the hatch usually comes off the best and timed the trip around what should have been a falling barometer.

It turned out that the television weatherman and the newspaper were both wrong—as they often are in mountainous country—and we arrived on the river at 9:30 in the morning on a bright, sunny, bluebird day. But the hatch turned out to be a good one anyway. The little flies weren't "boiling out of the riffles," as someone told us they'd been doing the day before, nor was the water "fuzzy with mayfly wings," but some flies hatched and some trout ate them, which is all you can ask for.

In fact, I've come to prefer hatches like that. There are enough mayflies on the water to get the trout interested, but not so many that your own little trout fly gets lost in the crowd.

The hatch started early—about 10:00—and, with a few dead spots, lasted until almost 5:00 that afternoon. I caught fish in the morning, broke around noon, found a pod of spawners and caught a great big one on a streamer, then went back to the dry flies. I can't say how many trout I caught, but I'd lost count by the middle of the day.

A.K., on the other hand, was having a pretty slow time. He was getting some strikes, but he seemed to be having a hard time hooking the fish.

He thought he'd figured it out when he checked his hook and found that he'd ticked his back cast on a rock and broken the point off, but when he changed to a good fly the fish still managed to elude him. It was one of those days when something—no telling what—was out of sync.

Finally he said to me, "They seem to be striking short," and I said, "Funny, I haven't noticed that."

A.K. did manage to land a few trout, but not many, and

on the ride home that evening he said to me, alluding to The Curse, "This was your fault."

And then, sure enough, it happened in reverse the next time. A.K. and I went back a few days later and met Ed on the river. It was another sunny day that was supposed to have been cloudy and, once again, the bugs came off unexpectedly well, except that this time they started later in the morning.

While we were waiting for the hatch to begin, I waded up into the shallow riffle where I'd landed that big spawning rainbow last time and caught another one just like it, only a little bit bigger. Ed waded over and took a photo of the fish. It was a large one, as I said, and the first trout of the day between us. I thought maybe it was going to be okay.

But then when the hatch came on and the trout started rising nicely, I found that I couldn't catch the fish, even though Ed and A.K. seemed to be doing well enough. I was using the right pattern—a #20 Blue-winged Olive parachute—and I was getting some strikes, but I just couldn't hook the fish.

I started setting up more quickly on the strikes—a sign of panic I exhibit automatically when I'm missing them, even though I know that's usually wrong. (As an afterthought I checked the hook, which was fine.) Then I started taking deep breaths and trying hard to slow down, you know, going for that imperceptible hesitation that's too long if you actually hesitate. I must have been on the right track because I felt a few fish and even had one or two on for a second or two before they threw the hook. I began to get that helpless feeling that there's one, single way to do it right hidden somewhere in a thousand easy mistakes.

Naturally, A.K. was hauling them in like a commercial fisherman.

Finally I said to him, "They seem to be striking short today," and he said, "Oh?" as he released a fat, fourteen-inch rainbow.

I did finally manage to land a handful of trout, two or three as I remember. A.K. and Ed, trying to be kind, allowed as how they'd done okay, although I had personally seen A.K. land maybe fifteen or twenty trout.

I guess I kind of expected this; what I didn't expect was that I'd break my bamboo fly rod.

There's no amusing story here, the rod just snapped cleanly in half below the ferrule while I was casting. I wanted to believe that I'd just thrown off my tip, but I'd heard a crack and, although I'd never broken a rod before, I knew what that had to mean.

Naturally, there was a photographer present. The guy had just wandered downstream wearing waders, carrying a camera and a small net, but no rod. He was catching mayflies and taking pictures of them. He saw me break the rod and watched me splash out to retrieve the tip, but when I glared at him he politely turned away. All I could think of was, any competent photographer would be tempted to capture a moment like that on film, and if this guy did I was going to have to throw his camera into the river.

The next day I took the rod down to Mike Clark, who'd made it for me almost ten years ago, to see if he could fix it. When I laid it on his workbench he said, as if he'd just found his favorite dog hit by a truck, "Aw, it's number thirty-three." (The serial number is actually 833, which, in Mike's system, means it was the third rod he made in 1983.)

He said he could repair the rod easily enough if I didn't mind it being about an inch shorter in the butt section, which wouldn't noticeably change the action. I said that would be fine.

As for the cause, we both knew that I had dropped the rod into its aluminum case too hard a number of times, damaging the joint between the bamboo and the female ferrule, which is precisely where it broke. Bamboo may be magic, but it still obeys the laws of physics. All Mike said about that was that it was a nice clean break. It almost sounded like a compliment. I expected a lecture on the proper treatment of a fine fly rod, but Mike just muttered something about pearls before swine and said he wouldn't charge me for the repair.

Luckily, Ed had a spare graphite rod along that day and he let me finish the afternoon with it. I didn't catch any more fish, but my heart wasn't really in it either, so at least I had an excuse.

On the drive home A.K. was jubilant about all the fish he'd caught, but he got serious just long enough to say he was sorry about my rod.

On our last trip to the Platte we were pushing our luck a little. It was the third week in February. The flow was decent for that time of year—about ninety cubic feet per second—but it was too early for the first mayflies, too early for the scuds, and reports said the usual late winter midge hatches hadn't really started yet. The day before, I'd called Ray Sapp at the Colorado Angler fly shop—a guy who's more likely to catch fish on the Platte than most—and asked him how the river had been fishing. "Weird," he said, which was not encouraging.

The February midging can be wonderful when it happens, but you have to be philosophical about it because there tend to be more slow days than good ones. You'll often spend eight or nine chilly hours on the river and maybe tease up a trout or two at best while getting your dues paid.

This is a safe trip, though. That is, if you get into fish at a difficult and spooky time of year, you've done something that at least approaches being extraordinary, and if you don't, that's pretty much what you expected, so you can congratulate yourself for being right.

And anyway, in late winter it seems only proper that you haunt the river for a while before things really start to happen. If nothing else, this qualifies you as a genuine local, so when some tourist turns to you on a pretty summer evening and asks, "Is it always this good?" you can say, "Nope."

This last time, we drove to Deckers, where the river was full of the previous night's glaze of bankside and bottom ice, now broken off, largely turned to slush and filling the main currents. Ten minutes down the road at Trumbull it was the same, or maybe a little worse.

Trumbull, a real town of maybe twenty cabins, seemed entirely deserted, as it often does in the winter. The only signs of life were a handsome black Lab and a dopey-looking basset on patrol. They stood in the middle of the road and watched us approach in the pickup as if they'd never seen a motorized vehicle before.

This ice floe, locally known as the slush hatch, only happens on mornings that are warmer and brighter than usual, and it makes the water unfishable. Trout won't rise through slush (bugs probably won't hatch through it, either), and even if fish are feeding under the surface, you can't get a nymph down to them. There's nothing to do but wait. Usually the river flushes itself clear by late morning. In the meantime it looks lonely and uninviting.

We drove back up to the Deckers bridge because the ice clears sooner upstream than down. There were a few other fishermen around, either sitting in their cars or rigging up slowly to kill time. The bar and restaurant at Deckers wasn't open yet, but the little worms and cold beer store was, and we got some fresh coffee there.

When the ice finally cleared, we got in at a favorite pool not far upstream from the bridge and started to fish. There were no rises and no flashes of trout feeding underwater, so this felt like the beginning of one of those long hauls where you cast and cast on automatic pilot, waiting for something to happen, living with the idea that it probably won't.

I don't mean to imply that we were depressed or anything. This is just a kind of fly-fishing—the kind where the odds are against you—and it's actually one of the better ways to spend a winter day.

I tied on a #20 South Platte Brassie, twisted some lead wire

onto my leader to sink it and started fishing in a deep hole.
I hooked and landed three trout on three successive casts,
each one a bigger surprise than the last. A.K. was amazed.
So was I, although I tried not to let on.

I was fishing the same rod I'd broken there almost a year
before, which I now think of fondly as Old Number Thirty-
three. Mike's repair was flawless, the rod does in fact cast
just the same as it always did, and I've come to see that missing inch of bamboo as a barely perceptible, but honorable,
scar. It's still one of my favorite rods, and I might even like
it more now than I did before.

Over the next half hour or so I caught four or five more
trout from that same hole, and then it went dead, as if someone had flipped the proverbial switch. A.K. had missed a
couple of strikes, but he didn't land any fish.

For the rest of the day we went through the obligatory motions. We drove back to a place just below Trumbull to check
on another favorite pool and found a guy fishing in it. I
walked past him twice, saying hello both times, and A.K. sat
on the bank near him for a while making a big show of re-
building his leader. We gave the guy every opportunity to
leave or say, "Come on, there's room for all of us," but he
didn't, so we fished some other water and then drove back
upstream.

By late afternoon it had turned cold and cars full of fishermen began passing us as they headed north up to the main
highway and home. I started thinking in terms of packing it
in, and I think A.K. was also leaning in that direction. But
then there was a short flurry of activity, just a few trout rising to a few tiny midge flies in two pools. A.K. missed two
strikes and I caught one small brown trout on a dry fly. Then
A.K. said something about hamburgers and one beer before
the drive home and that was the end of it.

There's a specific etiquette to this. The guy who didn't
catch fish must not whine or complain or offer excuses, and
the guy who *did* land a few (whether it was through luck or

skill) is not allowed to either preen or engage in false modesty. I've been on both sides of this often, and I don't know which is harder.

When we walked into the Deckers Bar we went straight to the wood stove to warm our hands. A blond woman turned around on her stool and said, "It's not that cold out, is it?"

"It is when you've been standing in the river fishing all day," I said.

"Jeeze," she said, "that's nuts. You guys must be from Texas or something."

There was a moment of silence during which any of the four other people in the little tavern who were Texans could have spoken up, then the woman said, a little shyly, "Well, *ah'm* from Texas."

She said she hadn't been to Deckers in many years, but had spent some great summers there as a little girl playing, climbing the hills and "terrorizing the fishermen." She'd been sitting there all afternoon playing ballads on the jukebox and talking about the old days with the bartender, who I think would be a little too young to remember.

I almost asked the woman about the two old mounted trout above the bar. Over the years—out of idle writer's curiosity—I've asked dozens of patrons and a handful of bartenders in this place about those fish, and have always gotten the same answer. It's believed they were caught from the very river you can see from all but two or three stools in that bar, but no one knows when or by whom.

These elderly stuffed fish are yellowed now, with slack jaws and curling fins, but once they were big, lovely, twenty-inch rainbows. Now they're just proof that trout have lived here for a long, long time, and that some people, at least, have been able to catch them. I almost asked the woman about them because she'd spent part of her childhood there and might know some history, but I stopped myself in time. Having talked with these nice Texas ladies before, I knew what her answer would be. She'd say, "Stranger, how old do you think I *am?*"

After we'd ordered our burgers and beers, the woman said, "Well, did you guys catch any fish?"

A.K. nodded toward me and said, "*He* did," and then he grinned. This was the properly gracious thing to say, but the smile was a little too wide. He was thinking, "Next time it's my turn."

7

In the Woods

Most stories about big game hunting are deceptive to the point of being untrue. That is, there's usually much more action in the story than there was on the actual hunt. It's not as bad now as it used to be, though. If you're old enough, you'll remember the lurid illustrations on the covers of outdoor magazines showing a hunter about to be devoured, gored or stomped by a different game species every month. The animal is only a few steps away—in full charge, drooling horribly or blowing snot—and the hunter, though surprised and off balance, is either chambering a cartridge or drawing a large Bowie knife. Things look grim, but there's the off chance the guy will come out of it alive.

A friend of mine refers to this as the "wild animals are trying to kill you" school of pulp art. Even when I was young and impressionable, I knew it was crap.

The fact is, a hunting trip is sometimes punctuated by a fabulous success, a horrendous failure or even something as unlikely as a misfire, but mainly it's days of standing, walking or sitting quietly, doing nothing obvious, in a state of mind that borders on meditation. This is how it's done, but it's not the stuff of thrilling narratives.

You'll usually see the species of game you're after, although often it's out of range, running, screened off from a clear shot by trees, or it's the right species, but the wrong sex: does instead of bucks.

In this last case you kick yourself for not having applied for a doe, or "antlerless deer," tag before the deadline four months ago. Maybe you spaced it out because it's hard for you to stop in June, when the fishing is just getting hot, to think about the October deer hunt. Or maybe you just couldn't get straight about *where* you were going to hunt and, since limited licenses here are for specific game management units, you had to let it slide.

Or maybe every few seasons you can't quite bring yourself to go through filling out an application form and entering a computerized drawing—always calculating the preference points you've accumulated from previous drawings or the ones you might get from this one—just in order to hunt one of the People's deer on the People's land. Putting together a good application now can be like figuring out your income tax and, in certain frames of mind, it's just as insulting.

But that's not your problem now. Now you're in the woods carrying an antlered license bought at the last minute from a hardware store, going to great lengths to blend into the environment; to be there, but not there, in what you know to be the finest hunting tradition. This takes either concentration or the thoughtless lack of it, and it's not something many of us get much practice at. Fishing takes patience and focused attention, but it's not the same as deer hunting. Neither is grouse shooting, or hiking, or bird watching, or mushroom gathering or politics or any of the other things you can practice until skill comes out your ears. I know some very good deer hunters, but I don't know how they got that way doing it for one week out of every year.

Sometimes in the spring or summer, when I'm just out for a walk or the fishing is slow, I'll spot a deer and try to sneak up on it, but something is missing. My ears aren't ringing with adrenaline, and the deer, though alert and suspicious, seems to understand that it's the off season and I'm just fooling around, which is true enough. I know that if this was October and I had a rifle under my arm, it would all be different.

I do a lot of what they call "stillhunting" because even now, in my mid-forties, I often lack the patience to sit absolutely motionless on a stand for hours on end.

Stillhunting is not exactly what it sounds like: You don't just sit still, you walk through the woods very slowly and as silently as you can (that is, with great stillness), taking a few cautious steps, then stopping to look and listen to everything around you.

No, that doesn't describe it properly. You move in deliberate slow motion, like in tai chi. Imagine that someone is watching you: In the space of five minutes you've gone twenty yards, but they never actually saw you do it. Okay, maybe not, but *imagine* that.

No, don't. Imagination is distracting. Get it into your head that you must see and hear everything, but disturb nothing. To stillhunt properly is to stand perfectly still while walking.

It's amazing how the distance you travel in even a single slow step can change your whole perspective. I don't know how an entire 250-pound mule deer buck can hide behind an aspen tree no bigger around than your arm, but I know he can—I've seen it.

You've just stood there for five minutes checking out every trunk, branch, twig and needle in the woods, then you take one step and there's the deer, looking right into your eyes, both ears trained on you like radar dishes. You're not acting like a normal human, so he doesn't exactly know what you are, although he's beginning to suspect something.

The trick now is to cock the rifle and raise it to your shoulder slowly and gracefully enough that you can get off your shot before the animal vanishes. A place to rest the rifle would be nice, but, although you're in a thick forest, there is no tree handy at the moment.

I've found it can be helpful in this situation to sink down on one knee or, better yet, drop slowly to a full sit. Not only is this a better shooting position, but I believe the deer thinks you're lying down, which, to him, is a curiously nonaggressive gesture. It puzzles him—sometimes he'll even take a cautious step in your direction to see what you're doing.

But that's a whole other story. That's the drama and excitement that, as I said, is rare. Your main occupations are slowing your pace, reducing noise and motion to a minimum and picking the forest apart piece by piece with your eyes and ears. You're not expecting to see a whole deer standing there like a field guide illustration, you're tuned for a glimpse of a white butt, an ear, a brownish-bone-colored antler, the line of a gray-brown back that looks like all the other rocks and logs, except that this one has no snow on it.

That's what you're looking for, although mostly you see birds, squirrels, hares, porcupines, maybe a fox or coyote, and as the days go by, if you're doing it right, you begin to appreciate what the woods are really like, that is, what they're like when you're not there.

Some years the forest may be lousy with coyotes. You'll

hear them at night—sometimes a long-eared or great horned owl will answer their calls—and after the first good snow you'll see their busy tracks everywhere. I'm told that coyotes are much in evidence during the hunting seasons because they're cruising around feeding on the entrails left by hunters who have field-dressed their deer and elk. You'll see ravens doing that, too, but you may never actually see the coyotes.

There may be blue grouse around, and you'll naturally consider shooting them for camp meat, although you should resist that because the report of a big-bore rifle—or even the crack of a .22 pistol—will blow a two-hour stalk. If you want grouse, you should *hunt* grouse. Now you're hunting deer.

Okay, so where are they? That's the big question. I've met hunters who seem to know, but each one of them has a slightly different theory. Some like to hunt hard in the evenings and early mornings when deer are moving between the places where they feed and the spots where they bed down. The mule deer we hunt in the western mountains aren't as habitual as whitetails, but if they're feeding in a certain meadow, there will be more or less logical routes to it along a ridge or through a saddle.

This will be stand hunting. You find a spot where you're fairly well hidden, but downwind and with a good view, and then just sit there doing your best to become a rock or stump. I don't much care for this, as I mentioned, but the rule of thumb is, when the deer are sitting still, you move, and when the deer are supposed to be moving, you sit still.

Often you'll see more deer during the season than at any other time because there are lots of people in the woods pushing them around, sometimes without knowing it. In that sense, it can be better to have loud, dumb hunters out there with you than good, quiet ones, although I don't know anyone who would consciously make that choice. In some cases where animal rights nuts have gone out in season banging pans and blowing whistles to scare the game, hunters have

worked around them, using them as beaters. Or so I've heard.
If you didn't care how you got your deer, I suppose it could
work.

Over the years, what you think you know about deer is
colored by having other humans in the woods. I once hunted
in some special muzzleloading deer seasons not far from
home. I liked the antique strangeness of the old rifles, the
fact that you had just the one shot with at least a couple of
minutes' reloading time, but mostly I was tempted by the
limited number of hunters out early in the fall, before the
regular rifle seasons.

I'll be hunting in something resembling natural conditions,
I thought, with the deer doing what they normally do instead
of being pushed around by crowds of other hunters. Then,
after a few days out without seeing any animals, I was thinking, Okay, but what *do* they do when no one is around?

I finally did shoot a deer with a muzzleloader, but it was
during a regular season. That fall I hung the .50-caliber cap
lock rifle on the wall—where it looks real pretty—and got
what some friends enjoyed calling a "real gun": a .30-06 with
a scope. I realized that handguns, bows and muzzleloaders
are for hunters who are so skilled they must always impose
greater restrictions on themselves to keep things fair. I'm not
that good.

The satisfaction of deer hunting comes not so much from
killing something as from being in the woods in a funda-
mental way, that is, as a participant rather than an observer.
The same is true of small game hunting, fishing, or mushroom gathering, but a deer is a large piece of meat and to
hunt one is to intend to cause what seems like a big death.
Even if you're only thinking of what you may have to drag
back to the road, it seems pretty serious. That's why I've
never shot an elk. They're not only more difficult to get than
deer, they're just too damn big.

Interestingly, the most practical state of mind for deer hunting is one of calm receptiveness, or about as far from blood-thirsty as you can get. You enter a stand of spruce and fir that looks and feels like an abandoned railroad terminal on a cloudy day: an apparently gloomy place that's cool in warm weather and sheltered from wind and snow when it's nasty.

A patch of this dark timber looks quiet and brooding from the outside, but if you sit absolutely still in there, or stillhunt through it for, let's say, two hours, you'll find that the trees are full of small, drab-colored birds, and that in breezes so slight you can't feel them the trunks of the trees creak and squeal like the doors of crypts in 1930s horror movies. It can take half of those two hours just to reorient your flawed human sense of what "silence" means.

Pinecones sometimes drop of their own accord, making thumps on the spongy ground that sound like hoofbeats, or rather, a single hoofbeat. This can leave you holding your breath, waiting for the other shoe to drop.

Little pine squirrels that you weren't aware of will suddenly break into a startled chatter, and this can be loud enough to stop your heart. The same little guys crashing around in dry leaves can make a racket like a bear rolling a log.

If the wind picks up a bit, there will be a shower of dead, rusty-brown needles that sounds like rain. Rain itself sounds like gravel being thrown against a blanket. Dry snow hisses, and wet snow sizzles like frying bacon.

Of course you can't be still forever—at least I can't—and eventually you'll begin to think you should hike another mile along the ridge and try it there, or go have lunch, or you'll just decide to break the silence on general principles. With those first few careless steps the rustle of your clothing is deafening. You walk twenty yards, step out into a grove of aspen and it's like someone switched on the lights. You've stepped back into your skin, and it will take a few more minutes to get used to it.

•   •   •

For the last several seasons, DeWitt, Ed and I have hunted deer in a rough part of a somewhat obscure big game unit on Colorado's West Slope, one of those places where doe tags go begging because the area is too rugged and not glamorous enough for many hunters.

There are some elk and plenty of deer here (including some big, handsome bucks) but they're widely scattered through steep, rough country, some of which is wilderness area where vehicles of any kind are forbidden. In short, you have to work hard for your animal—both before and after shooting it—so there aren't too many other hunters around. And what hunters there are tend to concentrate in the easier terrain, thus running many of the animals into the harder country where *we* hunt. Yes, we do feel sort of cagey about this.

And it doesn't hurt that DeWitt and his wife, Julia, have a snug little cabin up there. Having a warm, dry place to sleep on the deer hunt is downright luxurious.

Last year the party consisted of me, Ed, DeWitt and Julia. Actually, Julia only came up for a few days because she was busy with work and a graduate degree. Still, she didn't want to miss the hunting.

I enjoy hunting with Julia because she's good company, she's a good shot (she carries her father's old .30-06) and she shatters stereotypes, which is always fun. When we mentioned to a group of hunters who were staying nearby that DeWitt's wife would be arriving a day or two later, one of them asked, innocently, if she was coming up to do the cooking. The three of us glanced at one another, imagining what would have happened if this guy had asked Julia that.

The hunting conditions were tricky that year. There was no snow down for tracking and the country was dry, with lots of brittle aspen leaves and crackly pine needles on the ground, so stalking quietly was almost impossible.

I tend to start off sharper some years than others, and this time it took me a while to get into the proper head. I spent most of opening day wandering around the steep aspen benches and lodgepole pine woods where I'd shot my deer the season before. I tried to stillhunt, but several times I caught myself crunching loudly through the dry leaves and duff at a sauntering, game-scaring pace. We'd come up a day early and taken the obligatory hike to look things over—either to scout for sign and plan strategy or, as DeWitt says, to say hello to the country before you get down to business—but I still hadn't relaxed into the place yet.

I tried sitting a few times along wide, well-used game trails, but I was convinced that the deer weren't moving in the daylight, so I couldn't muster even the little bit of patience I have access to.

That evening I did take a stand at a good-looking spot. Two game trails converged in a saddle leading down to a grassy meadow. There were fresh scat and tracks showing that deer had fed there recently, and this was the only logical, easy way for them to come down off the mountain on that side. It was a perfect spot, but the only way to hunt it was to pick a place, become motionless and stay that way.

So I brought a book. This is a trick Julia uses and I thought I'd try it. We're both restless hunters who have a hell of a time sitting in one place quietly for, say, an hour and a half waiting for a deer to come along. Julia said that a book keeps her quiet and in one place long enough. Two years ago she shot a deer with a paperback novel open on the rock beside her without even losing her place.

Naturally, there are pitfalls here. I hunkered down about an hour and a half from dusk with some short stories by Raymond Carver. I got a little too engrossed in a piece entitled "Where I'm Calling From," and when I finally thought to look up the doe had already gotten way too close: no more than thirty feet away. Just that little movement of my head spooked her.

The story, like most of the others in the book, was about how heavy drinking can ruin a marriage.

Ed refuses to read on a stand, even though he's at least as

restless as I am. He feels that trying to fool yourself like that is futile because you're always in on the joke from the beginning, not to mention that flipping a page is like waving a flag. Instead he quiets himself by practicing meditation, or what he calls, "that old Zen stuff from the sixties."

Of course there's a pitfall there as well, which I pointed out to Ed. You'll see deer if they're there to be seen, but if you're meditating properly you may also come to realize that shooting one and not shooting one amount to about the same thing in the grand scheme. This can cost you your predatory edge.

As it turned out, we hunted up the deer we got by stalking them in daylight under what to me are the most difficult conditions. DeWitt's big buck was lying in some dark timber below a quartzite ridge. My doe was bedded down in tall grass on the edge of a broken aspen grove. I believe neither of these deer knew a hunter was there or that things were about to go wrong for them.

When I shot the doe I felt the usual jarring mix of emotions: a combination of something like surprise and elation, followed by a moment of sadness and, let's say, gratitude. Then I went to find DeWitt because it was a big one and I couldn't drag it all the way out by myself.

I like hunting with this group in part because we can talk about things like the sadness and the gratitude without feeling self-conscious. In the company of some hunters, that stuff goes over poorly.

Usually by the time someone shoots a deer we've been out long enough to have exhausted the latest media crisis. That year it was the idiocy with Clarence Thomas, Anita Hill and the U.S. Senate. Julia brings a refreshing perspective to these things because she doesn't pay much attention to the Big News, preferring to busy herself with more immediate puzzles that actually have solutions. When she walks in on the conversation and asks, "Now who are Clarence and

Anita?" you see the simplicity of it. You say, "They are two
people in Washington, D.C., who both may be lying."

"Oh," she says, "what else is new?"

Then there's time to talk casually about the inseparability
of life and death, joy and sorrow, skill and luck, hard work
and good food and so on. We fry thin slices of the current
fresh deer liver with onions. This is a casual, little, old ritual
having to do with pride and thanks, and it's the only time
liver ever tastes good to me. Then we drink some wine (De-
Witt is in charge of selecting the wine) and Ed says to me,
"Maybe you'd do better on a stand if you read something
more cheerful than Raymond Carver."

Another thing I like about this group is our feeling of community. When we started hunting together a few years ago
we agreed, in one of the shortest important discussions I've
ever been part of, to split up whatever we got so that everyone would come home with at least some meat. It was just
an obvious, practical thing to do, but I've come to really like
the sense of community that's formed around it. I'm hunting
for everyone, and they're all hunting for me.

Sometimes at a game dinner someone will ask, "Now did
you shoot this venison yourself?" and I've noticed it's as
pleasant to say, "No, it was a gift from some friends," as to
be able to say, "Yes, I did."

You'll sometimes run into hunters (older ones, for the most
part) who say they no longer care if they get a deer or not,
that they just enjoy the hunt, and that, in fact, killing an animal is when the fun stops and the hard work begins.

It *is* hard work, and I know it's possible to get enough of
that, and if you're hunting to prove something, I suppose it's
possible to get it proved, finally, and then just want to hang
around camp doing the cooking and splitting wood.

For my part, I still want to get one, that's why I'm out there,
although I have gotten to the point where it's okay if I don't.

Not entirely acceptable, mind you, but okay. That's another way of saying, *I wanna get one.*

And I guess I also enjoy that poignant mix of emotions. If I try to live by a single principle, it's, "Do no unnecessary harm." This principle actually comes into play more often when I'm contemplating punishing someone or exacting revenge. If I take an insult too seriously, I have to wonder if maybe the insult wasn't accurate, or consider that I'm getting arrogant, as in "who is *he* to say that to *me?*" In other words, before I say something like, "Now listen, you asshole . . ." I am forced to think, Is this necessary?

When it comes to shooting one deer a year for food, I've already decided that it's the correct thing to do: a matter of necessary or at least useful harm. The chore at hand is to do it right, which is what separates sport from mere food gathering—that and the fact that I wouldn't live as well without deer meat in the freezer, but I *would* live.

So what I want is a clean, humane, one-shot kill, and I won't fire at an animal if I don't think I can manage that. Mostly this is a matter of understanding your limitations and being properly humble. I'm a decent rifle shot out to about 100 yards, which means if I see an animal at 250, that's not my deer—and you don't want to shoot one that is not, somehow, yours. Consequently, I hunt dark timber and broken woods where the skills I have are right for the habitat.

If I get a deer early in the season I'll still stay on for a while. Technically, that's so I'll be there to help the others haul out and skin *their* deer, but really it's because I don't want to leave yet. It's such a great place to be: The country is pretty, the cabin snug and comfortable, the talk good.

Sometimes I'll have an elk license, even though I have little interest in killing an elk or, maybe more to the point, in quartering one and hauling it out of the woods. More likely I'll bring a shotgun and wander around the woods with it on the pretext of hunting grouse. There's a pretty good trout stream not twenty feet out the back door of the cabin, but I never bring a fly rod because this is a hunting trip.

In seasons when I don't get one early, I find I become more instead of less patient as the days go by—at least up to a point. This is not exactly resignation, it's just that I know I'm doing what I'm supposed to as well as I can, and I also know that desperation is not a productive attitude.

Maybe later in the week, with the season beginning to wind down, I'll drive the ten miles or so to the nearest little store for provisions and gossip. You know this place: one gas pump outside; deer antlers nailed above the door; one small, unpainted room containing stale bread and single-serving cans of pork and beans at prices three times what they'd be in the nearest town.

There's an excited, slightly paramilitary atmosphere in the store, and some other hunters are hanging around in their orange hats and vests, some of which are newer and brighter than mine. It occurs to me now and then that if I hadn't grown up dressing like this every fall, I might feel a little bit ridiculous.

These guys have three elk and a deer hanging in camp and they feel pretty good about it. Not crazy or anything, just good—satisfied.

One of them asks me, "Have you killed anything yet?"

"No," I say, "but it's sure nice to be out in the woods."

They don't reply to that. They just look at me as if I was the quarterback of the Denver Broncos and I'd just said, "Sure, we lost the Super Bowl, but what the hell, it's only a game."

8

Scotland

*F*or once it was exactly as I'd pictured it, which is something a fisherman doesn't get to say very often. There were real castles and slate-roofed stone cottages scattered around a green river valley, ghillies in knee-high breeches and leather vests, a water bailiff in a deerstalker cap who slept days and only ventured out in the gloaming when poachers were about. Hundreds of pheasants strolled the fields and roosted in the oak forests where the deer live, waiting for the driven shoots in the fall.

We dressed in jackets and ties for dinner, drank the good whiskey they don't export to America and, of course, our party of five fished hard for six days and caught one fish among us.

We were fly-fishing for Atlantic salmon on a private river in Scotland in late June—a good river at a pretty good time of year, by all accounts—but this was what everyone had told me to expect. "Even if you do everything right, you might not catch one. *You've got to understand that*," they said, or words to that effect.

The thing about Atlantic salmon is, once they've run out of the sea and into their home rivers to spawn, they don't feed. As always, there's a logical reason for that. If these big salmon came into the rivers hungry, they'd eat up all the salmon parr from the previous year's spawn and wipe out the whole next generation of fish. Perfectly logical, when you think about it.

So a salmon comes into a river carrying enough nutrients in its tissues to last it many months, its digestive system ceases to work and physical changes occur in the fish's hypothalamus that bring on what Lee Wulff called "a loss of appetite or nausea." This is not the moodiness you sometimes see in trout; these fish really don't eat, so they're really not supposed to bite.

This is something a fisherman has to think hard about and get firmly in mind.

Hugh Falkus, in his inch-and-a-half-thick, three-pound *Salmon Fishing: A Practical Guide*, says, "What is surprising is not that salmon are hard to catch, but that any are caught at all." Every salmon-fishing book I've ever peeked into has said something like that, usually right near the beginning so you won't get the wrong idea. This has been known to work, but you've gotta understand that it's not *supposed* to work, okay?

I'd never fished for Atlantic salmon before and in the end it was the very unlikelihood of catching one—the exciting weirdness of that—that finally attracted me to it, or at least that's what I thought. Looking back on it now, I realize I didn't believe I'd actually get skunked. I thought I'd experience the epitome of sport everyone talks about, work hard, confront frustration and otherwise take my lumps, but I also thought I'd eventually catch a fish.

I should have known better, because the sport is lousy with stories not just of blank days but of entire blank seasons. A man in Scotland told me he'd caught five salmon the first time he'd fished for them (that's unheard of and it cost him a fortune in scotch at the pub afterward) and then he didn't catch another fish for three years.

Once a story like that is told among salmon anglers, everyone else trots out *their* story. It's a form of competition, the winner being the guy who went the longest without a fish, but still didn't give up.

When I said okay, sure, it's just that I couldn't remember the last time I'd fished for six days straight without so much as a strike, I was told, "A bad week is nothing, lad, nothing a'tall."

This river had been held privately for the last six hundred years—the whole river, not just a piece of it—but an English company had recently bought the fishing rights from the estate and was offering them for sale on a time-share basis: one week in perpetuity for seventy thousand pounds, or about twice that many American dollars. There were six of us altogether: five American writers—Tom, Scott, Don, Clive and me—plus Laine, Clive's photographer (although Laine might have said that Clive was *his* writer). Some of us were magazine staffers, some were on assignment and others were freelancing, but that was the story: time shares on a salmon river in Scotland, a cultural hybrid of an idea that was supposed to make Americans dive for their checkbooks.

Since only five rods were allowed on a beat, Laine couldn't fish, but he said he wouldn't have even if he could. He thought fishing was insane. He hated the boredom, couldn't stand getting wet or cold and didn't care much for fish anyway, except maybe kippers. Turning to Clive he said, "Remember when I covered that sea trout story with you? Night after miserable night in the freezing rain, in a leaky boat, not even the paltry excitement of catching a fish, and having to put up with you the whole time."

But, he added to the rest of us, as a professional photographer he could, and would, take pictures of anything, and they'd be damned good, too.

We began downstream at the Downie beat. Our ghillie, Matthew, put me on The Breaches pool and asked to see my flies. I had a single box of brand-new wets: Copper Killers, Thunder and Lightnings, Undertakers and General Practitioners that a man who'd fished Scotland had recommended, plus a brace each of Jock Scotts and Green Highlanders for local color.

"Did you tie these?" asked Matthew.

"No, I bought them."

"In America?"

"Yeah, from a place called Hunter's."

"Well," he said, "they're terribly pretty," as if prettiness was a nice enough touch, but it wasn't going to make any difference.

He broke off my tippet and retied it—because no guide anywhere likes *your* knots—then selected a small General Practitioner on a double hook and tied that on for me, too. There's no reason in the world for an Atlantic salmon in a river to bite any fly, but among the people who fish for them this way there's still something that clicks, making one pattern look better than another.

Laine was photographing all this: the American fisherman being instructed by the Scottish ghillie with Croiche Wood as a backdrop and good morning light. He hated to get wet, but to achieve the right angle he had waded into the river up to his shins in tennis shoes.

There are subtleties to Atlantic salmon fishing (there must be, there have been so many thick, ponderous books written about it), but when you don't know what you're doing, you do what you're told. In this case, you "work the water."

You start at the top of a pool, make a quartering downstream cast, fish it out, take a step downstream and do it again. The fly is fished on an across and downstream swing, so you end up covering the entire pool in what would look, in an illustration, like a series of sickle-moon-shaped stripes about two feet apart.

At the bottom of the pool you get out, walk back to the top and start again. You're fishing with a floating line, so your unweighted wet fly swims very shallowly, within an inch or two of the surface. Of course the salmon usually lie much deeper than that so, as unlikely as these fish are to bite in the first place, they have to make the full commitment and move for the fly. It seems like an outside chance, but that's how a gentleman fishes.

I asked if maybe a guy shouldn't concentrate on places where salmon would likely be lying. "Yes," said the ghillie, "that would be all right."

"So where do you suppose that would be?" I asked.

"Oh," he said, making a gesture that seemed to include the whole pool, "all through there."

You think the ghillie should have more to tell you about this, but he doesn't, or at least you assume he doesn't because you don't see much of him. I had assumed the ghillie was there to be helpful, like an American guide, but then I was from out of town.

I fished down the pool, letting the fly hang in the current for a minute or so at the end of each swing because sometimes a salmon chases it and hits it when it stops. I fished through the pool maybe five times. On the third or fourth pass two men on horseback trotted into a clearing on the far bank and sat watching me. I waved, but they didn't wave back. That was the most exciting thing that happened all morning.

A friend of mine said he'd been salmon fishing once and had actually enjoyed the mindless, repetitive nature of it. He didn't mention whether he'd caught a fish or not, which means he didn't. He also said he can spot the Atlantic salmon story in which the writer got skunked by the first paragraph. "It's all about the castles, cottages, ghillies and deer forests," he said.

We were staying at the Cruvies House, a large cottage on the river at the bottom of the Falls beat, complete with a tile-floored fishermen's changing room and a heated drying closet for waders and rain gear. The river side of the dining room had a line of French doors looking out on the cruvies themselves—a set of V-shaped stone dams with cribs used for netting salmon in the old days. The old days in this case dated back to the 1400s.

Lunch was served at the hut on whatever beat we happened to be fishing, but we ate breakfast and dinner in that room overlooking the river, usually with Dick, who was president of the company that owned the fishing rights.

Dick was charming, quick with a joke, always in charge in an evenhanded, British way and, he said, a student of all things American, even to doing most of his riding on a western saddle. He gently instructed us in the ways of salmon fishing—more the etiquette than the technique, although some of us were weak on both—and occasionally corrected our speech.

When the subject of priests came up, someone asked, "What do you mean by a 'priest'?"

Tom said, "In this context, it's a little weighted club you use to bonk a salmon on the head to kill it."

"I wouldn't put it quite that way," Dick said.

"Why not?"

"Because here 'bonking' means 'screwing.'"

He also tried to explain cricket, but gave it up when I said I didn't even understand baseball.

These dinners were at least three courses, prepared and served by Jane, who is probably the best fancy meat and potatoes cook I've ever met. She was self-employed, working sometimes for Dick and sometimes for other parties of salmon fishers who rented cottages in the valley. She was the best cook in the county, she said, and these rich folk, being used to the best of everything, often bid against each other for her services.

One day I got to talking with one of these guys, a wealthy sport who was a tenant on half a dozen of the country's best salmon and sea trout rivers, and who seemed to stop fishing only long enough to do a little driven grouse and pheasant shooting. He seemed like a nice man—if nothing else, he was spending his money right—but he also gave off a certain air that's hard to describe: almost as if he thought he could have you beheaded if the mood struck him. Anyway, he'd told Dick he wanted to meet some of these American writers who were such hard-core fishermen they weren't even stopping for tea.

He asked me about the Frying Pan River in Colorado, which he'd heard about.

"Now, when you go over there and camp for a week," he said, "do you bring your own cook from home or do you engage someone locally?"

I had to tell him that, as far as I knew, there was no one like Jane in Colorado. He winced slightly when he heard the name. She was cooking for us that week, which apparently meant he and his party were getting by on cold porridge, stale bread and cheap wine in bottles with screw caps.

I liked Jane immediately—we all did—and not just for the great food she put out. She was a genuine wild Highlander who pointedly took no crap from anyone, addressed no one as "mister," liked to refer to us as boys, her boss included—although she was younger than most of us—did not engage in false modesty and managed the kind of dignity that allowed her to serve meals without seeming like a waitress. She made you want to hang out in the kitchen, even though (or maybe because) that seemed to be frowned upon.

Jane could do a great impression of a midwestern American accent, complete with appropriate dialogue ("Hey, Bob, get a load of this here church"). She said, "You can always spot Americans by their wide arses and small heads." She also happened to be pretty: willowy, but not anorectic-looking like a model.

I noticed right off that Scott was hanging out in the kitchen more than the rest of us, but I thought maybe he just had a domestic streak and was pumping her for recipes.

I think that cottage is the most comfortable place I've ever stayed while fishing. We each had our own big, homey, high-ceilinged room with a huge bed, down comforters and a private bath (with English plumbing, but then nothing's perfect). My room looked out on the river, and since the nights were only chilly, I slept with the windows open. We put in long days fishing, drank some and ate large meals, but I still think it was the river that put me away each night. The sound of it hissing through the cruvies had the same effect as morphine.

Laine seemed happy enough for a day or two. We fished methodically and he took pictures. Fishermen casting, or wading, or tying on a fly while standing conveniently in front of an ancient churchyard. He'd pose you carefully one minute and then tell you to just do whatever it was you were doing the next.

At first he'd be saying, "Yes! Great! Perfect!" all the time he was shooting, but then he started muttering things like, "No," "No good," or "Nope, not weird enough."

"Not weird enough?" I asked.

"Any idiot can take a picture of a man fishing," he said. "Anyway, the magazine likes weird photos. That's why they hired me. And by the way," he added, "is someone going to catch a fish soon?"

Don did catch a fish the next day when we rotated up to the Falls beat. It was about eleven o'clock in the evening, just dusk that far north, and he was casting to a salmon that had boiled several times more or less in the same spot. Tom said, "Now that's a taking fish," and Don had started down the bank saying, "Let's see."

A "taker" is the salmon everyone is looking for. It's the one fish in God knows how many that, for reasons of its own, will take your fly. This may have to do with habit or the memory of feeding, aggression, curiosity, playfulness, the fish's freshness from the sea, time of day, time of the most recent tide, weather, water conditions, fly pattern, a defective hypothalamus or some combination thereof. It's a mystery but, since it ultimately has to do with sex, the odd moodiness of it also seems vaguely familiar. One thing is clear: A taking fish is defined after the fact. As Matthew told me, "A taker is the one you caught, if you catch one."

"How do you know that's a taker?" I asked Tom.

"Just a guess," he said.

And then Don caught the fish, a lovely fourteen pounder. It was what they call a "bright fish," fresh from the ocean with sea lice still on it and shiny as a chrome bumper. We all ran down to watch him land it and take some photos, even though the light was almost gone. All of us except Scott, that is. He hadn't come out with us after dinner. In fact, it seemed as if he vanished about the time Jane went home.

Come to think of it, Laine wasn't there either. Earlier that day he'd begun mumbling about taking a different approach and needing some props. No one had seen him since.

It turns out that Laine had driven into the nearest town and, after hours of haggling, had rented an ornate old grandfather clock from the suspicious owner of an antique shop. When we came in that night it was lying in pieces in the front hall.

"What's it for?" Dick asked at breakfast the next day.

"I don't know exactly," Laine said, "but, you know, it's about time shares, so I felt I needed a large clock."

Dick nodded thoughtfully. There *was* a certain logic to it.

We were late getting on the water that day because it took an hour or more to drag out Don's salmon and pose it and him in every way any of us could think of. Then someone else would have to pose with it so Don could get some shots. After all, it was his fish. And then you'd have to do everything both with and without the ghillie, who would have been happy to get done with this foolishness and get on the water. "This is a good deal of excitement over one fish," he said.

Laine followed us around for another day and a half, taking candid shots, posing each of us in turn at the scenic Back of the Castle Pool, fooling with fill-in flashes and reflectors and generally waiting for someone else to catch a fish.

It seemed as if all of us fishermen were waiting for the same thing. That's what it feels like: the repetitive, almost hypnotic cast, drift, step; cast, drift, step. You're not so much fishing as you are waiting for a fish.

Of course as writers we had other things to think about. Presumably Don had at least the germ of his story, but what about the rest of us? Fishing with fishing writers is strange enough anyway, but when almost everyone is getting skunked and searching for a new angle, the conversation can get pretty weird. You'll make some idle comment like, "Well, it's a pretty spot anyway, with those castle towers poking up above the trees," and someone will say, "Yeah, man, there's your lead."

Scott seemed to be sublimely above all this, taking the lack of fish philosophically, but he *was* under some strain. In the evenings he'd say he was bushed and was going to turn in early. Then in the morning we'd come down to find him in the kitchen chatting quietly with Jane as she cooked breakfast. But it was all just a little bit *too* discreet, and peeking into his room was too much of a temptation for some of us. Sure enough, the bed hadn't been slept in, not that it was any of our business, of course.

Then later, out on the river, Scott would turn up missing

again, only to be found curled up in the tall grass sleeping like a baby. When he'd get caught at it he'd say something like, "Gee, this salmon fishing is more strenuous than I thought."

One day Laine and some of the others decided to photograph one of the great lunches we were having catered at the fishing huts. (The angle everyone seemed to be working on now had more to do with cuisine than fishing.) We hauled the table outside—for natural light and the river as a background—and Laine, Tom and Don began arranging food, wine, wicker picnic baskets, two-handed fly rods and Dick into the perfect *Gourmet Magazine*-style composition.

Of course no two photographers think alike, so there was some disagreement about what should go where. I didn't have an opinion, so I was standing off to the side, out of the way. Scott sidled up beside me and asked, quietly, "Ever hear the expression, 'high-speed goat fuck'?"

I said, "No, but I like it."

Someone commented that the only thing missing was a salmon, at which point Matthew jumped into his little pickup with the dog kennels in the back and roared off down a dirt road. I thought he'd gone to the cottage to get Don's fish, but instead he came back in ten minutes with a nice grilse (young salmon) of about seven or eight pounds. The fish was so fresh that, although he'd killed it, it was still twitching.

Someone said, "Perfect!" but I thought, Wait a minute, if the ghillie knows where a fish can be caught that easily, shouldn't he be putting one of us on it? One of us like me, maybe?

It was just an idle thought. The grilse did complete the photograph and Dick, who'd been standing at the head of the table holding a glass of wine and wearing a frozen smile, seemed relieved to finally hear the shutters clicking.

"May I drink this now?" he asked.

• • •

On the fifth day we trudged back to the hut on the Home beat for lunch and Dick, who looked a little confused, said that before we sat down to eat, Laine would like to see us all up at the cruvies, in waders, with our rods.

We drove up to the house, and when we got out of the van I heard bagpipes. They were faint, but unmistakable.

"Scott," I said, "do you hear pipes?"

"Yeah, I do," he answered sleepily, "but I wasn't gonna say anything."

It seems that the same day Laine had rented the clock, he'd also engaged the services of a piper; an authentic Highlander in a kilt, bearskin hat, dagger in his boot, the whole catastrophe. By the time we arrived Laine had the clock sitting in a shallow riffle out in the river with a battery of lights and reflectors trained on it. Don's salmon had been resurrected and was lying on the bank. It was a couple of days old now; its eyes were glazed, its jaw was locked open and it was starting to look pretty dead.

The piper was standing back in the trees to keep out of the light drizzle. He was playing his heart out because, as near as he could figure, that's what he'd been hired to do.

I've always loved the sound of bagpipes—played well, they make me want to either cry or fight—but I noticed Matthew cringing every time the guy launched into another tune.

"Don't you like this stuff?" I asked.

"Well," he said, "a little of it goes a long way, doesn't it?"

I thought, of course: punk rock, spiked hair, pale girls dressed in leather. Our immediate surroundings notwithstanding, this is still the twentieth century.

Over the next two hours, in a steady light rain, Laine posed every possible combination of one grandfather clock, one piper, one dead fish, five fishermen and one bored ghillie with a long-handled landing net. He was the only one not wearing rain gear and he was soaked to the skin.

"This is it!" he kept shouting. "Time! Salmon! Scotland!" Then he'd rush to adjust some small detail. "What time should the clock say?" he asked of no one in particular. I guess we were watching genius at work.

Dick was a little puzzled by all this, but he wasn't shocked. Over the last few days you could see him slowly getting used to us. We asked some impertinent questions, but then we were writers. Sometimes our language was a little rough, especially after a few drinks, and we seemed to prefer the company of the help instead of the rich sports, but then we were Americans.

I didn't think Dick cared about Scott "taking up with the cook," as he put it, until we rotated back up to the Falls beat on the last day and Scott wasn't there because he'd disappeared with Jane again. Dick didn't say much, but he was clearly scandalized, so I asked, "Does this really bother you?"

"Who's bonking who isn't my business," he said, "but one simply *does not* give up a salmon beat."

As near as I can tell from the little bit of reading I've done, fly-fishing for Atlantic salmon is based on the premise that anything that can happen will, eventually. There are many theories on when, where and on what fly pattern salmon will bite, but, by all accounts, no theory produces fish often enough to be proven true.

Even the experts speak in italics. There *should* be a fresh run off this last tide; this fly *should* work in this pool, if only because it has, off and on, for generations. When salmon aren't caught—which is most of the time—these people take a kind of sly comfort in the fact that, given the circumstances, you really ought not to be able to catch them at all. Meanwhile, the accommodations are posh, the food is good, the booze flows freely and there's the general feeling that things are as they should be.

This would seem like an expensive snipe hunt except that you see fish. Some are boiling and porpoising, others are jumping to dislodge sea lice. Jumpers won't bite, they said, and that was the only statement about salmon I heard that wasn't followed by several contradictory footnotes.

You put yourself through this because some fishermen say catching an Atlantic salmon on a fly is as good as sex, even though you know in your heart it isn't. I agree with a friend of mine who says that if fishing is really like sex, then he's doing one of them wrong. Still, there do seem to be similarities.

For one thing—as the salmon fishers tell it—either you catch a fish way too soon, before you're fully able to appreciate it, or you have to wait much longer than you think you should have to, so that when you finally hook and land one the elation is tempered by a profound sense of relief.

And, of course, repeated failures don't lead you to the logical conclusion; they only whet your appetite.

Back at the cottage in the evenings, the more experienced salmon fishers—Clive, Dick and Tom—would hold forth. The river flowed by just outside the French doors. It was clear but, because all its water had first filtered through peat in the Highlands, it was slightly whiskey-colored in the deep pools. The way to catch salmon, they said, is to keep your fly in the river and be of good cheer. They didn't seem to understand it either, but they still appeared to possess a kind of wisdom.

It reminded me of when I was a kid and some grown man would decide to take me aside and give me the kindly lecture on women. He'd fall into this vague, humorous mode, trying not to let on that, although he had considerably more experience than I did, he still didn't know what the hell he was talking about.

Apparently, the genuine salmon fisher takes pride in his acquired tastes, strength of character, fine sense of irony and apparent craziness, which he and a few other aficionados know isn't really craziness but, well, something else entirely. As a trout fisherman, I used to think I understood that, but salmon types look down on us trouters as dilettantes. I mean, we catch what I now think of as quite a few fish. Small ones by comparison, but fish nonetheless.

• • •

We fished for six days and took Sunday off, not because we were tired or discouraged, but because it's illegal to fish for salmon on Sunday. I asked why, but no one knew. It's just always been that way. We took the rented van and, with Dick as guide, drove up into the Highlands to look around. All of us except Scott, of course. By now, no one had to wonder where Scott had gone.

I kept dozing off in the backseat. When you've fished long and hard and it's become obvious that you're not going to catch anything, it's a relief to finally stop and let it all sink in. As it sank in, I tended to lose consciousness.

On the flight over, Tom had gone into that old salmon-fishing refrain: *You've gotta understand you might not catch one,* and I'd said, maybe a little impatiently, that I understood that. "You understand it intellectually," he said, "but if you really *don't* catch one, there's a hump you'll have to get over."

Right. I could see that now. You have to learn to see yourself not catching fish as if from a great theoretical height.

I also realized that I liked it and that I'd probably do it again, and then again if I had to, until I finally hooked and landed one of the damned things. To prove something, to be able to say I'd done it and because I knew it would be beautiful somehow; not like sex, of course, but in a way so weird that that's the only fair comparison. I also knew that this is how a life can be ruined by sport, and just as I was dozing off I had a vision of myself on a street corner with a tin cup and a sign reading, "NEVER COULD CATCH AN ATLANTIC SALMON ON A FLY ROD—PLEASE HELP."

The next morning, Dick drove Don and me to the airport at Inverness. Clive and Laine had left early, and Tom was staying on for a day and then heading to Russia, where there were bigger, dumber salmon that hadn't seen six hundred years' worth of flies. We could only guess at Scott's whereabouts. He hadn't been seen for at least a day and a half.

Dick was in a good mood. He said he'd enjoyed having us. "There was a lot of laughter this week," he said, "much more than usual. To be honest, some of the people who fish here are a little stuffy."

Then he asked, "Do you think we'll see Scott at the airport?"

There was some shrugging and throat clearing, and I thought, Would *I* be at the airport?

Dick drove on quietly for a minute and then said, "Well, if he turns up in the next few days, I'll see if I can find a little job for him."

(Author's note: Five months later, in Virginia City, Montana, Scott and Jane were married.)

9

The Storm

*I*t was a good spring to be self-employed and a fisherman. From early April all the way into June the weather had been flipping back and forth more wildly than usual, even for Colorado—warmer when it got warm, bitter when it got cold, snowing when it should have just rained—but if you averaged it out it still amounted to what you'd expect: Things were waking up and, when you could catch it right, the fishing was good. But if you wanted to fish in the proper conditions, you had to be in a position to drop everything and go when things fell into place. At those times when things weren't as right as you thought, it was good if that wasn't your only day off.

The rocky weather muddied the trout streams early, broke some freshly leafed-out cottonwood trees with wet snow, pleased some farmers, worried some ranchers and brought complaints from spring turkey hunters, as well as the usual pissing and moaning from big-haired local television newscasters who can't understand that the American West is not the Bahamas.

Local bass fishers weren't whining because it's undignified, but they did say the largemouths never really got on the spawning beds "in a meaningful way."

That's where it stood when Steve, Larry and I went to a private bass pond out east to try to re-create an earlier performance. We'd fished there a week before, dodged the weather successfully for a few hours and caught some good-sized fish before getting rained out. These bass were in exceptionally fine shape—chunky and heavy—and we thought maybe the aborted spawn had saved them from getting beat up and then having to recover. In the long run, there'd be a missing generation of bass in the waters where they manage to reproduce naturally, while in the short run the fish were fatter and prettier than usual. In the interest of playing the ball where it lay, we thought we'd try them again, even though the odds are against pulling it off that well twice in a row.

On the long drive out to the pond, things seemed to be shaping up into a nice enough spring day. The air was warm and there were scattered puffy white cumulus clouds against a blue sky so perfect it looked like the underside of the universe. Driving east, away from the foothills and out toward the Plains, the country always strikes me as enormous, but in that first bass-fishing weather it seems bigger yet, as if doors you'd forgotten you'd closed had been flung open. The conversation was louder than usual, both from happiness and because the windows in the pickup were rolled down.

The big, dark thunderstorm to the south looked as if it would blow past us by quite a few miles. Judging by the angle of the gray veil of rain trailing behind it, we figured it

was going roughly west and a little north, while we were going east and a little south. There was no telling how far away
it was without knowing its size, but I claimed—based on its
purplish-black, almost eggplant color—that it was a great big
one and, therefore, many miles off. With the air of a man
who has just heard what he wanted to hear, whether he's
completely convinced or not, Steve said, "No question about
it," and quickly moved to a different subject: canoes, I think.

But by the time we got to the pond the storm had changed
direction (or we'd guessed wrong in the first place), and it
looked as if it was wheeling toward us. We stood watching
it for a few minutes and agreed that we'd just get clipped by
the extreme eastern edge of it—a cool, twenty-minute squall
at the worst.

A breeze was already ruffling the pond, and it seemed the
smartest thing to do would be to cast streamer flies from the
bank, working the rough water in the shallows where fish
might come in to see what was being stirred up. Little fish
to eat the bugs, big fish to eat the little fish—the old by-the-
book theory that works more often than most. We were still
in sunlight, but the sky was troubled and the bright air felt
chilly and damp. This was no time to launch Steve's and
Larry's belly boats, let alone my fragile little canvas canoe.

By the time we had our rods strung up, the wind had gotten a little too strong for fly-casting. Steve tried, but no. When
you have to hold your hat on your head with one hand and
dodge your streamer fly, it's too windy. But the weather
wasn't threatening enough yet to drive all three of us into
the cramped cab of the pickup, so we took a walk. It was
something to do, it would be bracing and we wouldn't get
so far from the truck that we couldn't make it back in one
good dash.

This pond lies in a low spot in an expanse of classic western high plains country. At first glance it's dry, open, rolling
and scrubby—dramatic and severe—but of course it's pop-
ulated by most of what are now the appropriate creatures,
native and otherwise, many of which are attracted to the scat-

tered, cottonwood-lined ponds. This is where you see herons, ducks, geese, pelicans and ibis and where the white-tailed deer you never see in daylight seem to grow up out of the ground at dusk.

This is settled, owned country where it's almost impossible to step off the road bed without permission and not be trespassing, but it's also pleasantly empty: few buildings, few paved roads, a couple of scattered oil wells. The fabled Rocky Mountains are back on the western horizon looking lower and closer than they really are.

This is not great pheasant country, but we saw two and heard at least another cock. The cackle of a cock pheasant sounds like the squeak of an oil well in need of lubrication and also the sound a loose, rusty barbed-wire fence makes in a gusty wind, but you do learn to tell the difference after a while.

As we strolled past a windbreak of trees, a mourning dove flapped off across the ground doing the injured-bird distraction routine, and we were able to find the nest. There were two young doves in it, just starting to get flight feathers.

There were all the usual magpies, cowbirds, blackbirds, starlings and such. And there was a western tanager and also a blue grosbeak, which was a new bird for me, one I'd always wanted to see.

I've always liked the way birds chatter when weather is moving in. They're like humans then, pointing out the obvious, having conversations like, "Hey, look." "Yeah, I see." Not long ago I read that the Tlingit Eskimos in Alaska think owls say, "Get under trees," when a storm is coming, and whenever they say that a storm *does* come.

The wind was really up by then and we decided to head back to the truck, which was the only real shelter in sight. For a while the sky had been blue with lit-up clouds almost yellow above the purple underside of the storm, but suddenly it was gray and somber, with just a line of bright weather to the north. I was carrying my hat because it wouldn't stay on my head, and I could feel a few raindrops on my bald spot.

Back at the pickup we ran into a pair of big peacocks. They came out of the trees to meet us, clearly used to people, but then realized we weren't who they thought we were and shied off a little. We knew the guy who owned this spread raised some exotic birds, but we didn't expect to see them two miles from the house.

We stood by the truck watching the edge of the storm slide in toward us. At a distance it looked almost stationary, but right above us the disk of cloud was scudding by pretty quickly. The tall, slate-gray part of the storm went right to the ground about two miles off in solid curtains of rain. On the edges we could see either filmy rain squalls or the beginnings of funnels, we couldn't be sure which.

The center of the storm was full of lightning, and we counted the seconds between the flash and the crack to see how far away it was. Not far. We noticed that the peacocks had hunkered down under the truck, so we decided to get into the cab ourselves. We were starting to get wet and the temperature seemed to have dropped by about twenty degrees.

It was a wonderful storm: The sky was dark, the rain was in nearly rhythmic, pulsing sheets that laid the cattails down flat. The pickup was broadside to the wind and it was high profile, a big, square '78 Ford with a topper on the bed and a canoe on top of that. It caught the air like a sail and rocked on its springs, making a sound like, oddly enough, a cock pheasant. To the south and west was a purple wall, but what we could see of the sky behind us to the north was clear, so we were just into the edge of this thing.

At the height of it there was some small but dangerously driving hail. Larry pointed at the roof of the cab and asked me if I was worried about my canvas canoe up there. I said, "Maybe a little, but I'm not gonna go out there and do anything about it."

"Yeah," he said, "that's probably wise. I was just asking."

We had a good time sitting in the truck for about forty-five minutes, not talking much because of the din of wind, rain, hail and thunder; just taking the occasional small nip from the flask of Southern Comfort and now and then yelling, "ISN'T THIS GREAT?" or "SON-OF-A-BITCH," or "IT'S GET-TING KINDA COLD, ISN'T IT?" It occurred to me that this is something you have to look for in fishing partners: the quality of uncomplaining acceptance, or at least the ability to have a decent time even when things aren't going too well. To put it another way, you don't want to be trapped in a storm with a whiner.

Then I thought I saw something on the water, a funny movement, a shape that wasn't waves: something. I turned on the windshield wipers, which helped only a little. We were parked facing the pond, maybe ten feet from the bank.

I said, "Are there fish rising out there?"

Steve said, "No."

Larry leaned forward, squinting, and said, "I think I see what you see, but I don't know what it is."

I turned the wipers to high and we all leaned up over the dashboard. Yes, it was hard to see, but there appeared to be greenish-bronze shapes moving at the surface. Not logs, not weeds, too substantial to be water shaped by the wind, too green to be carp (and there are no carp in there that I know of), too big to be panfish. I opened the door and leaned out. Before I could even focus I was soaked all down the right side, but I could just make it out.

"God damn it," I said, "there are bass rising right in front of us."

Larry opened his door, leaned out for a second, then slammed it closed again and said, "Yeah, maybe."

Steve sat between us holding the Southern Comfort and said, "No."

"Get out and look," I said.

"No."

• • •

We got on the water when it was all but over. The storm had bashed off to the northwest and the thunder had gone from loud cracks to dull, retreating rolls. Gusts of cool wind were blowing themselves out in the trees. The pond was nearly still and the sun was back out, even though a thin drizzle was still sifting down from a great height. The peacocks seemed blissfully unconcerned. They were high-stepping through puddles of clay-colored water and pecking at seeds and bugs. The air was sweet and magical, and I thought of a line written years ago by my old, mad poet friend Marc Campbell: "Peacocks strolled beside the lake/Like illuminated manuscripts."

I launched my canoe while Steve and Larry were getting into waders and flippers and skidding their float tubes down to the water through the dripping grass. The canoe's caned seat was wet from splattered rain, but there was no hail damage to the leathery hull.

I made a quick, ten-minute tour of the pond just to feel the little boat glide, passing Steve and Larry twice as they paddled their tubes over to the good bank. I like belly boats when I'm in one, but when I'm next to them in a canoe I feel like a swan.

Then I tied off to a bleached stick and flipped a little cork popper into the flooded timber. After a few casts I had a big bluegill and then, out of thicker cover, I got a heavy, fifteen-inch bass. I held him in the water for a few seconds before letting him go and thought, That's what I saw boiling around in the shallows during the storm; same shape, same color, only bigger than anything I've ever seen or caught here before.

It wasn't what you'd call useless information, just too small a piece to too large a puzzle, like when, once every two or three generations, it rains frogs. Okay, but if you *want* frogs, there are better ways to get them than standing in the backyard with a bucket. A friend tells me that trying to figure out things like this is like teaching a pig to sing. It may be interesting, but in the end it's a waste of time and it annoys the pig.

We all caught some fish, but the storm had cooled things off, so there wasn't the usual flurry of feeding right at dusk. We fished until dark anyway, going the last half hour or so without a strike. The pond was like a smooth disk by then, but rainwater was still dripping from the trees and spattering in the shallows near shore, making a narrow band of muddy water. Both the bluegills and the bass seemed to be cruising along the edge of it, right where the water cleared.

The closest town was closed up and pretty much deserted, but Larry said he knew of a good, cheap Mexican joint that might still be open. It was two blocks off the one-story main street, with a warehouse on one side and railroad tracks on the other.

"La-something," he said.

"Cocina?" I said. (Half of all Mexican restaurants in the west are known as "The Kitchen.")

"No," Larry said, "La-something else."

They had just closed when we walked in, but when all three of us looked pitiful the guy told us to sit down while he saw if he could still whip something up. When he came back with some beers, he nodded at the bass bug stuck in Larry's baseball cap and said, "You been fishing?"

"Yup."

"Where?"

We told him, vaguely: "A pond sort of near Such-and-Such."

"That tornado out there give you any trouble?" he asked.

"Not much," Larry answered.

"Well," the guy said, "we still got some enchiladas."

CHAPTER

10

Getting Lost

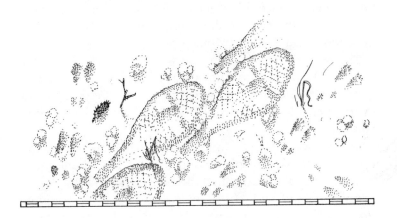

*E*d Engle and I were hunting snowshoe hares in a stretch of northern Colorado not far from where I live that's a little too low to be properly "in the mountains" the way tourists mean that, but still a bit too high and rugged to be considered the foothills. It's not remote, but it's nicely in between, so it doesn't get a lot of traffic.

Technically, this is where the foothills and montane forests blend together at an altitude of around eight thousand feet, with the mixed textures of juniper, red cedar, Douglas fir, aspen and ponderosa, lodgepole and limber pines. Not all together, of course, but shading together, with odd patches and stands here and there. It's all thick, western woods. There are no meadows, and even small clearings are rare.

This transition zone is one of the richest parts of the mountains around here and my friends and I are automatically drawn to it. There are lots of different trees and shrubs, and lots of wildlife. This is where the cottontail rabbits begin to thin out and the snowshoe hares take over. There are scattered but dependable pockets of blue grouse up there, deer, elk, plenty of coyotes and bobcats, the odd fox, two kinds of squirrel and so on.

This is roughly the altitude where brown and rainbow trout begin to give way to brookies in the streams, and it's where snow lies on the ground all winter, even though it melts off between storms lower down.

This area is close to home, so we can be casual about it. We take day trips into it for trout in the summer and fall, grouse in September and hares in winter. We don't know every inch of it, but even in strange new parts it feels familiar.

It was a weekday late in the season when Ed and I drove up. I don't think we'd planned in advance to go hunting. As I recall, one of us had called the other with half the day already gone and said, "Let's get the hell out of here and go *do* something." I think it was Ed, because he was working on a book that winter, and when he's deep into a big project, he sometimes explodes out the door with a firearm or fly rod, depending on the season.

This was a cold, heavily overcast day with a good base of snow down and a fresh cover falling lightly, straight down, without a breath of wind. This is perfect, of course, because every track you see that looks fresh *is* fresh.

This was an area we'd only started hunting that season, but it had turned out to hold lots of hares, so we'd been in there four or five times, not enough to really come to know the place, but enough to have become a little bit casual about where we were. You know how that is.

Ed had discovered this spot the summer before when he moved up from Colorado Springs to work for the Forest Service in the Boulder District. It's a sizable chunk of Forest land that, for one reason or another, most people don't understand to be public—including me until recently. When we took a mutual friend up there he said to me, "It's interesting that you've missed this for fifteen years or so and Ed found it in one summer."

"That's why I hang out with the guy," I said.

Ed and I left the pickup on the snowy dirt road, strapped on our snowshoes and waddled roughly south until the land began to fall off into the narrow east-west valley. Here we split up. Ed likes to hunt the aspen bottoms where the hares feed, while I prefer the ridge sides where the animals' forms are. A "form" is the somewhat sheltered spot where a hare will sit out the time he's not feeding. Usually it's next to a pile of rocks, a tree, a stump or something else that will break the wind.

My theory is that the hares eat in the mornings and evenings and often at night, even in winter. (Actually, it's not *my* theory, it's what the books say.) I think they then hop up onto the hillsides where they sit in form through most of the day, resting and digesting. At least that's how I hunt them, and it works as often as not.

Then again, the fact that Ed gets them down in the aspen bottoms means that this is somewhat short of the whole truth, not that the whole truth matters that much.

Anyway, I'll cruise a hillside not too far up from the brushy bottom where the tracks in the snow will be matted and crosshatched as if fifty animals had wandered through there the night before, although in fact, it was probably more like three or four. When I find a single track heading uphill in a more or less straight line, I follow it.

There's a certain logic to this. That is, there *will be* an animal at the end of the tracks; the trick is to pick out a fresh, readable trail and then be able to stay with it. On a calm, cold day after a fresh snow, it's not that hard, but all kinds of things can screw it up.

In fluffy powder, all tracks can look fuzzy and aged. A track left in wet snow that then freezes in a cold snap can be a week old and still look fresh. Wind can age a track in a matter of minutes, and so can falling snow, or old snow sifting down from the trees, or an hour of warm, high-altitude sunlight. A hare that's run from soft snow onto a crusty patch can seem to have taken flight, although if you look carefully you may find faint claw marks.

A snowshoe hare tracker pays closer attention to the condition of the snow than a skier, and he should also have a pretty good idea of what the weather was like yesterday and last night.

I've gotten fairly good at tracking, but there are still days when it baffles me, even though I may know, in an intellectual sense, what must have happened. I have learned to walk next to hare tracks instead of in them in case I have to go back and start all over again. To me it's like Spanish. Living here in the West for so long, I've picked it up a little bit, by which I mean I can order *huevos* and *cerveza,* and sometimes understand simple directions spoken slowly, but I can't read the poetry.

The tracking is the art, but the shooting can be pretty simple. If you've done it right—following the tracks with your eyes as far ahead as you can see, and then scanning the ground—you'll spot the hare sitting, and in thick woods the ranges are close.

I used to use a .22, but now, in the interests of class and sport, I carry a .36-caliber flintlock squirrel rifle, complete with fifty-five inches of tiger stripe maple stock. This thing is handsome, heavy and difficult to shoot, and there's some suspense inherent in the fact that sometimes it chooses not to go off. You'll never fully understand the meaning of the phrase "just a flash in the pan" until you've had your flintlock misfire on a hunt.

Anyway, the rifle saves me from having to admit that the shooting part of it doesn't require much skill.

Snowshoe hares really are amazing animals. Around here they live in the roughest country starting at, let's say, around seven thousand feet and ranging all the way up to the scrubby brush above timberline, although they seem to like forests best. They're active throughout the coldest months when they manage to scrabble out a living on twigs, buds and the bark of young aspens. They're also known to be fond of frozen meat and will gnaw on the carcasses of dead animals.

Because they live where the snow gets deep, they have evolved unusually large, fuzzy hind feet that act as snowshoes, hence the name. It's even been said that these hares gave the American Indians the idea for snowshoes, although that's probably just an informed guess.

In summer these animals are brown and look like oversized cottontails, but in winter they turn white for camouflage, and their primary survival tactic is to sit motionless while a predator just walks by. Their secondary tactic is speed, and they can really move. I've measured the tracks of running hares at as much as six feet apart.

The meat is excellent, although older animals can be a little tough and should be stewed or marinated. In many parts of Europe, wild hare is a delicacy, and it would be here, too, if we paid more attention to what we eat.

The glossy hair from the hind feet is used as wings on a trout fly called a Usual, and the under fir on the body is good dubbing for dry flies and nymphs. It's a pale tan color (only the guard hairs turn white), so it's good to dye or to blend with other colors for shading and texture.

Hares are everywhere in the right kind of habitat, but as white bunnies frozen on the snow, they're not easy to find. Once found, they can materialize, vanish or seem to fly low over the ground in a disturbingly ghostly way. They're great to watch, even while they're getting away.

I think the fascination I have with game animals, fish and birds is a kind of envy. They live in and with wild country in a way I can't with my technology, my need for comfort and my poor, slow, hairless body.

Here in Colorado, the daily bag limit on snowshoe hares is ten, but I can't remember ever getting more than three or four in a single trip, and one or two amounts to a good outing. In that way it's like fishing. It goes on and on—good, poor, occasionally fabulous—and some days it seems that this could last forever.

Not long ago a friend asked me if I wanted to go hunt bunnies with him in Wyoming. It seems he'd found this place where there were thousands of them. It was easy shooting, he said, and he and his friends had gotten thirty-five apiece on the last trip. (I didn't ask what the legal limit in Wyoming was, but I had to wonder.) Tales of slaughter can get to a hunter, but I said no. I told him that if I shot thirty-five of them, my freezer would be full and my personal bunny season would be over for the year. I'd rather get them a few at a time and keep hunting. It ends soon enough as it is.

So, Ed and I split up in the bottom to pursue our different theories. I'd hunted the two facing ridges a few times before so, just for a change, I decided to cross the valley, climb the next ridge and hunt the slope down on the far side. It would be a little piece of new country that I'd better see soon if I didn't want to wait until next fall. Sure, I could go up there after the small game season ended at the end of February and just take a walk, but I knew I wouldn't.

It took some doing to get where I wanted to be. It was steep going down and steep going up the far side. The snow was crusty under a thin cover of powder, so sometimes my snowshoes didn't bite and I'd slip. Of course a hare doesn't have this problem. In deep, soft snow he spreads his toes to gain surface area; on hard snow he brings them together; and on crust he digs in his claws. (You don't need to study bunny physiology to know this; you can see it clearly in the tracks.) Anyway, human-made snowshoes are neat and useful, but they're a poor approximation of the real thing.

On the top of the ridge—a place I'd never been before—the trees were shorter and the snow had been dusted off by the wind so that it was only an inch or two deep, polished hard and punctuated with bare, rocky spots.

Hares don't like it on the tops of ridges. There's nothing tender to feed on up there, and they like to be out of the wind when they're sitting in form. I also believe they use the deep snow on the slopes to get away from predators, skipping over the surface of it while the bobcat, fox or coyote that's after them bogs down.

I hurried over the top—snowshoes scraping on exposed rocks—and just before starting down into the deep, fluffy snow on the far side I heard the single, muffled crack of Ed's .22 rifle. So, he had a bunny. Ed is not the type to whang away at improvised targets while hunting. Nor is he the type to miss.

Once I was well down the far slope I turned to my left. That, I figured, would take me out the ridge more or less to the east. When it was time to come out, I'd simply climb the ridge again, drop over the other side into the familiar valley, and up the hill to the north would be the road. When I hit it, the truck would be to the left. Simple.

I hadn't shuffled twenty steps in that direction when I spotted a hare hunkered down stock still next to a fallen tree. Believing in his white camouflage right to the end, he just sat there and I shot him. Sometimes hunting is *not* a great drama.

I wondered if Ed had heard the shot. Possibly not. There was snow on the ground, snow in the air and a ridge top between us. And, for that matter, the muzzleloader makes a duller thump than the sharp crack of the .22.

It was late in the season, as I said, ten days until the end, in fact, and I had already eaten a number of snowshoe hares that winter. I wasn't exactly tired of them, but as I dressed this one out I thought maybe I'd make something special with him: roast him in sour cream and wine perhaps, or serve him fried with a goat cheese sauce. I've noticed that the fancy cooking starts late in the season.

A brace of bunnies would have been nice, but the hillside didn't produce. There were only a few old tracks fading in the fresh snow, and no other hares that I could find. Maybe there were no juicy young aspens down in the bottom on this side, or maybe the bottom was so far down there that the hares didn't climb this high on the ridge. I have come to think that the high ridges separate populations of snowshoe hares because the bunnies don't like to cross them, but I can't prove that.

I could have gone down the slope to see what was there, but it was getting a little too late for any more exploring. In fact, it was getting late enough to start thinking about heading back.

I'd gone about a mile to a mile and a half out the slope, so I figured I'd go over the top where I was, drop down into the valley, and then angle west and up on the far side. That way I'd cut either the road or my own tracks from where I came in.

So I did that: up the slope, across the windswept crest and then down the far side. I was swinging along—as well as one can swing along in snowshoes—supremely confident that I knew exactly where I was and where I was going.

About halfway down one of my snowshoe bindings came loose and I stopped to fix it. When I straightened up I looked over at the far ridge through the falling snow and it occurred to me that it was both lower and about three times farther away than it should have been.

Bummer.

I looked around. I don't know why, but I always look around at a time like that as if there's going to be a sign nailed to a tree saying "YOUR TRUCK IS THIS WAY," complete with an arrow.

If this sort of thing has ever happened to you, you know it represents a crucial moment. The difference between being lost and being just temporarily turned around is simply a matter of attitude. If you approach it as an interesting problem, you are momentarily disoriented. If you freak out, you're lost.

I figured a compass reading would be a good place to start, but after a few minutes of rummaging around I realized that the compass was in the pocket of the jeans I'd worn last time, and that said jeans were hanging over the back of a chair at home.

The check is in the mail; I'm from the government and I'm here to help you; the compass is in my other pants.

I had a pretty good idea of what I'd done. I must have walked to a point where the valley had swung south, making the ridge fall off to the east instead of continuing in that direction forever. Instead of making the 180-degree swing over the top, I'd made more of a 90-degree track, so I was going parallel to the road instead of toward it: east instead of north, looking across a wider valley at a hillside I'd never seen before.

That had to be it, right? I had never looked at a topographic map of the area so I couldn't be absolutely sure, and the sky was a uniform flat gray, so I couldn't locate the sun for a fix. But what else could have happened? All I'd have to do was follow the hillside around until the far ridge got closer and higher like it should be. That would head me west, and a right turn would point me north, toward the road.

That had to be it, but if it wasn't I'd be spending the night out. There was enough daylight left for one try, but not two. I wouldn't have died or anything. I'd spent two unplanned nights out in the woods in the past and hadn't died either time. I guess I had been a little worried and sleepless those nights, but in the end the worst part had been the embarrassment.

This time I even had a rabbit to eat, although it would be tough and dry, roasted over an open fire, no goat cheese sauce, no California cabernet.

The woods seemed profoundly quiet, although I could hear the almost imperceptible white noise of light snow sifting through pine needles.

Of course there was an easy way out of this. Behind me stretched my own snowshoe tracks that would lead nowhere but back to the truck. They were filling with snow, but that was happening slowly. Even dusted over, the trail was deep and wide enough to follow easily in the failing light.

So I backtracked. It added a mile or more to the hike, but

it was a sure thing. I found the road right at dark and Ed was waiting at the truck.

Ten days later, February 28, Steve and I went back to the same place one final time to observe the last day of the season. It was a low-key hunt, the most memorable part of which were some sets of tracks Steve called me over to look at. You could clearly see where a bobcat had chased a hare, at one point getting close enough to pull out a few tufts of his white fur amidst a jumble of footprints. The hare had finally gotten away, and the cat tracks seemed to just vanish in a grove of trees. We thought maybe he'd climbed one of them and we looked for him for a long time. We never saw him, but he could well have been up in there somewhere. These were tall spruce trees with their tight needles packed with snow. There could have been a bear up there and we wouldn't have seen it.

All this was very fresh, and we discussed the possibility of following the tracks of the escaped hare, but Steve said he thought maybe the bunny had paid his dues for today already and didn't deserve to be shot. That sounded reasonable. Maybe a small act of kindness is appropriate on the last day of the season.

Steve headed off to find another set of tracks, and I decided to go find the place where I'd gotten lost and turned back the last time. It took me less than a half hour to get there, and I walked right to it as if it was a familiar bus stop.

So, I had been right that day; I had known exactly where I was and had simply lost my nerve, opting against having faith in myself.

It was a rather pretty spot, actually: a pine-forested hillside with the trees spaced wide and parklike and a jumbled rock outcrop standing to what I now knew for sure was the west. But I didn't remember it as pretty when I was lost there. Then it was just a strange place, a single, useless coordinate, like one of those "you are here" markers without the rest of the map. If I was the lover of the outdoors I claim to be, I would have at least taken a second to think, "Well, wherever the hell I am, it's sort of a nice place."

Interesting. Something to think about during that long wait from the end of February until the fishing starts.

My old tracks were faint, but still readable. I could see where I'd come down the ridge, stopped to check the snow-shoe binding, paced around in a tight circle a few times, and then started back along the old trail.

Funny, I don't remember pacing.

11

On the Ice

*I*t was novelist Jim Harrison who said that ice-fishing is "the moronic sport," and he lives in Michigan, so he should know. Still, that's not entirely fair, because it actually takes some skill, patience, understanding and fortitude to do it right. (An actual moron would catch a few fish, but not many.) But at the same time, every fisherman sort of knows what he means. There's something about sitting on a frozen, windswept lake staring down that eight-inch-diameter hole that looks—at least from a distance—like the primitive equivalent of watching television.

For a long time the ice-fishing I did was out of desperation. As a kid in Minnesota, I went because the men went and I naturally wanted to be a man, although a little ice-fishing got me to wondering if I really wanted to grow up so fast after all.

Here in Colorado I got back into it because it helped fill those long, dark months when nothing much else was going on outside. It didn't exactly cure the shack nasties, but after a day of ice-fishing, sitting around the house being bored didn't seem so bad after all.

Once I was ice-fishing a big, flatland reservoir for perch and walleyes. I had a small pile of fish lying on the ice and it wasn't so cold that I was quite miserable yet, but it was still one of those dank, leaden days when the chill really registers as the absence of something. You stand there with hands in pockets watching the two shades of gray where the sky and the horizon meet, and if you're not careful you'll start cataloging your regrets.

I'd spotted an odd-looking bump about a hundred yards farther out on the ice and finally, just for something to do, I wandered over to see what it was. It was a prairie dog, frozen dead in a posture I really don't care to describe. I can't begin to imagine what he was even doing out of his burrow on a day like that, let alone half a mile out on a frozen lake.

If you spend a lot of time outside, things like this are like strange little gifts, in this case a simple illustration, without editorial comment, labeled, "Mortality: for what it's worth." It was getting late anyway, so I got my fish and went home where it was bright and warm.

As I've gotten older I see that there's a positive, bioregional perspective to sports like this that most objective observers would think are no fun at all. Throughout much of the world, the lakes freeze in the winter, but fish can still be caught through holes in the ice if you possess the old knowledge. Once, knowing about things like that was crucial to survival and even now it seems more than just interesting. It is a thing to do in the place where I live, so it's compelling. And if it's sometimes desolate and uncomfortable, well, as Gary Snyder says, "Life in the wild is not just eating berries in the sunlight."

•   •   •

That's how I'd come to think of the sport when I fell in with a couple of guys who were serious ice fishers. That is, they fished year-round, but they seemed to prefer doing it through the ice. When they caught trout from pretty mountain lakes in the summer with fly rods, they said they learned things about the fish and the structure that came in handy later, when they could walk to wherever they wanted to be on the lake instead of just casting from shore. I know, that's hard to picture, but there *are* different ways of looking at things.

These men also fished for trout in a style that was unfamiliar to me at the time. Instead of sitting on an overturned bucket watching a bobber—a pose that can suggest either prayer or the contemplation of suicide—you lie face down on the ice with a blanket over your head, look through the hole and watch the fish.

It's not as bad as it sounds. For one thing, you lie on a foam pad, and my friends had even designed a pad with a hole in one end to fit over the hole in the ice, stubby wings of foam on either side for your elbows and attached hoods. You carry your pad rolled up under your arm or, if you're going some distance, strapped to the top flap of your pack like a sleeping bag. When you get where you want to be, you bore your hole, place the pad over it and point yourself into the wind to keep the hood from blowing off. You're dressed for serious cold weather and the hood cuts the breeze, so it can actually be pretty cozy in there.

But the best part is how well you can see. These guys fish in no more than ten feet of water—usually less—and when the conditions are right it's like looking into a well-lit aquarium. You can see everything: individual grains of gravel, nymphs and scuds crawling on the live green vegetation and, of course, the trout. This is the most visual kind of fishing I've ever done and, although fishermen always say this, you really can have a great time whether you catch anything or not.

The right conditions include clear water, a day at least

moderately bright and a windswept lake where most of the snow has been dusted off. Too much snow dampens the light and things can get pretty murky down there.

For a fly fisherman like me, the actual fishing tackle is disturbingly simple: a small spool of monofilament line, a pair of clippers and a handful of jigs. That's it. It all fits neatly into one coat pocket, leaving both hands free to lug the rolled-up pad and an auger.

Although I claim to admire sparseness, I don't think I'll ever get used to this. True, a real outdoorsman carries only the tools he needs and depends more on cunning than technology, but I can't get it out of my head that if you want to catch lots of fish, you should have lots of stuff, or at least a varnished bamboo spool for your hand line.

Once you're in place and your eyes have become accustomed to the light, you lower your jig until it's about a foot off the bottom. Then you wait for a fish. (That last sentence should probably be followed by five or six blank pages to illustrate the potential weight of it.)

I'm calling the things you use here "jigs" because that's how I know them—small, lead-headed lures with their single hooks riding up—but I understand that some purists insist on calling them "ice flies," which I have to admit sounds better to the ear of a fly caster. I guess I sometimes grasp at aesthetic straws here, if only because fishing without a rod seems as if it should be illegal. Whatever you call them, they are usually nonrepresentational, tending toward clunky and heavy on the bright colors. My friends said it was hard to find good ones.

So I got some standard one-thirty-second-ounce jig heads and tied some flies on them: Hares Ear soft hackles, Zug Bugs and Damsel nymphs with heads painted to match the bodies and two-tone enamel eyeballs. They looked good, more like something a trout should want to eat, and I gave a hand-

ful to each of my friends. They were duly impressed. "Yeah,"
the one guy said, "*that's* what I meant."

The flies caught fish—suddenly they did seem more like
flies—but I have to say they never quite replaced the black-
bodied Tube Jigs or White Walleys that are local favorites.
When the pretty ice flies were finally all gone, I didn't bother
to replace them because I didn't have to. By then I had also
learned that a proper ice fisher buys his few sparse items of
tackle at the hardware store like everyone else. In one sense,
style is just style, but it does grow out of actual conditions
so it shouldn't be ignored. When you're ice-fishing, there's
no reason to get classy, and a couple of reasons not to.

But if the gear isn't especially snazzy, there are still plenty
of elegant little tricks to it that unfold slowly, even in the
company of experts.

One November we hiked into a high-country lake not far
from here. It seemed way too early to ice-fish, but my friends
assured me this is how it's done.

"Look," one of them said, "you go way up high early because the ice is safe sooner up there and because if you wait
too long it will be two feet thick."

Sure, that's obvious once you think about it, and there was
also an undertone of experience to it, as if two-foot-thick ice
was more than just a sterile concept.

I showed up for the trip with the usual gear, including the
auger, which one of the guys pointed to and said, "Don't
bring that."

"Why not?"

"Because you won't want to carry it where we're going."

The day was bright, clear and crisp—good shirtsleeve
walking weather. We slogged up a steep hill from the trailhead (not on the trail, this was a shortcut) and worked our
way west along a dry, rocky ridge. I knew it would be colder
up high, but a safely frozen lake still seemed unlikely.

We cut a trail and followed it uphill through open pine,

then denser spruce and fir. It was chillier in the trees and we hit the first snow at about nine thousand feet. It was just a dusting on the ground at first, but it got deeper as we gained altitude. When the snow was about ankle-deep, just enough to drag each step a little, we stopped to rest and pull on sweaters. Even with the uphill grind, it was getting brisk.

The last mile or so was agonizing. The snow had gotten knee-deep, crusty on top, powdery underneath. We took turns breaking trail to the top of a deeply forested ridge and then started downhill to the north. We'd put on the water-proof wind suits to keep from getting wet.

The steep pitch down to the lake wasn't long, but this was a north-facing slope and the snow was waist-deep in places. I'm convinced it couldn't have been negotiated without the help of gravity. Luckily, we could go back up though our own trail.

The lake itself was small, maybe ten acres, and set in a deep cirque. A little creek drainage fell off to the southeast, and to the northwest was a looming, distinctively horseshoe-shaped mountain. The mountain and the lake have the same name, and it's one I promised not to divulge.

The rocks visible above timberline were all but dusted bare, but down in the trees the snow was piled deep and undisturbed except for the odd tracks of pine squirrels and snowshoe hares. The lake, however, was swept down to clear, gray-blue ice and when we stepped out onto it we could feel the cold wind that must blow up there all winter long.

We chopped our holes with a short spud one of the guys had carried in neatly sheathed in an old, three-piece aluminum rod case strapped to the side of his pack. As I chipped away with the thing, he said to me, "Now when you break through with that, *don't drop it*," and I thought I heard the voice of experience in that, too.

The ice was perfect, four or five inches thick, hard as glass, and the guy had been right. An auger would have come in handy, but I was glad I hadn't tried to carry one in.

We only fished for about two hours. We weren't doing very

well and it was blisteringly cold up there. Even under the hood, packed in so many clothes I could hardly bend my elbows, I was beginning to shiver and the tips of my fingers were numb. The wind was a constant whistle and the edges of the hood popped like a flag. I began to long for the slog back up that snowy hill to the top of the ridge because I knew it would warm me up.

We only caught a handful of fish. I got one, a beautiful little ten-inch cutthroat with the greenest back and the reddest stripe I'd ever seen on a trout. When I hand-landed the fish through the hole, it felt warm.

As we were getting ready to leave, I made the mistake of taking my foot off my pad for a second. It sailed across the lake, piling up on the rocks on the far bank, and I had to waddle after it like a penguin. Coming back I thought, Someday I'll be telling someone how to do this; I'll say, "Don't drop the spud in the lake and hold on to your pad."

After we caught our breath at the top of the ridge, one of the guys said, "Sorry, it's usually a lot better than this."

I said it was fun and I had, after all, caught a fish. That's the polite response when a friend apologizes for the fishing, but it was true. I was in that state of grace that comes early in such things: still delighted that it even works, too new at it to think I could have done better.

It's not always that dramatic. Usually the hikes are shorter, and sometimes we fish within sight of the car because hardly anyone does this so there's no competition to speak of.

The small mountain trout lakes are always beautiful in winter in a forbidding kind of way, and at first it's always hard to imagine that anything is going on under there. But then you auger your hole and peer in and it's all still happening. Bugs crawl, trout cruise. They even work the shallow littoral zone just like in summer. It's the same element, just a little more inaccessible.

So there you are, face down, peering through your port-hole in the ice, waiting for a fish to come along. If you were fly-fishing, you could cruise the bank, casting in a pattern and watching the birds, or climb into a canoe and troll; if you were grouse hunting you could try another hillside; but drilling another hole is a big commitment. For one thing, it's too much like work. For another, the sand and grit that are always trapped in the ice of windy mountain lakes will quickly dull the blades on your auger, although if you have an allen wrench and a stone, you can remove and sharpen them.

It's permissible to twitch your jig from time to time to attract the attention of fish—a sharp, upward bump of about two inches followed by a slow sink is good—but it's best to go easy on that. Even under the ice, trout are touchy, skittish fish, and too much action on the lure will spook them, especially if they're close to it.

If you jerk the lure and spook a trout that's close, but still out of sight, you'll know it. Sometimes there's just a momentary current caused by the trout wheeling and swimming off, enough to move the jig a few degrees to the side and then let it fall back. A larger fish might stir up a little silt off the bottom, and the effects of a really big trout bolting look like those atomic bomb test films. First all the weeds lean in one direction, and then a blast of mud blows through. That was a six-pound trout that will probably not come back.

You're not supposed to talk while you're under the hood, on the premise that the fish can hear you, but at a time like that it's permissible to shout a muffled obscenity.

Sometimes a trout will sail into your cone of vision, casually inhale the jig and keep going—an easy strike—but more often the fish will materialize a few inches from the lure and hover there studying the thing, paddling his pectoral fins in a thoughtful way. He may eat it then, or he may swim off, only to come back a minute later to glare at the jig again from another angle.

At times like this you really want to give a little twitch to that jig—just to be doing *something*—but of course that's the one thing you shouldn't do. The trout seems very close; in some cases it may be only an arm's length away. You're looking down on its dark back, but you can easily count the spots and see the red stripe on the side of a rainbow or the orange flanks on a brook trout.

You feel like a voyeur. You notice that you've been holding your breath. Naturally, the bigger the fish the more unbearable the suspense.

When you hook a fish, you throw the hood off and lurch to your knees to play it. For a few seconds you're blinded by the sudden light and disoriented by being back in the air again. You had begun to feel as if you were really underwater with the trout. The hand line is clumsy, easily fumbled or fouled. All in all, there can be a good deal of confusion.

But it can be a long time between fish, and the excitement is mostly cerebral. From a distance, someone fishing this way looks like a frozen corpse, especially when, as often happens on these windy lakes, a little powdery snow has drifted up around him.

A season or two ago a carload of tourists in Rocky Mountain National Park spotted one of my friends fishing like this. They drove right down to the ranger station and reported a body on the ice with its head covered by a blanket. Clearly a mob-style execution—one of the things they'd come all the way out here to get away from.

12

Alaska

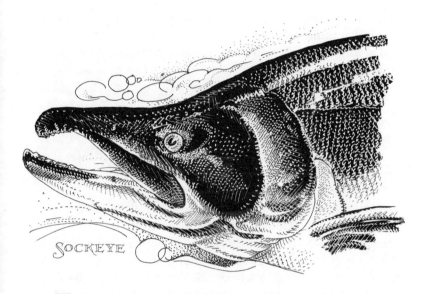

SOCKEYE

*T*he backcountry of Alaska is a perfect silence broken by the sound of motors: generators, outboards and especially the droning of float planes. Up there the single-engine plane is the equivalent of the pickup truck. Once you're away from the state's handful of roads—in the bush where the fishing is really good—a plane is your only way of getting anywhere, not to mention getting back.

I was in Alaska not too long ago with my friends DeWitt Daggett and Dan Heiner. DeWitt is a publisher and Dan is the managing field editor of an outdoor magazine (which means he manages to get into the field as much as possible). I'd never been to Alaska before and DeWitt had just moved to Anchorage, so this was a first good look around for both of us. Dan was the local boy with all the connections.

We fished from three different lodges—technically, two lodges and a hotel—and spent a lot of time in the air, which is standard procedure. There would be the flight in and then, most days, weather permitting, we'd fly out to this or that river in the morning to be left with a guide and maybe an inflatable raft or a boat stashed on site. Then we'd be picked up at a predetermined place and time to be flown back to the lodge in the evening.

Or what passes for evening. In the Alaskan summer there's a little bit of duskiness in the wee hours, but nothing those of us from "down below," as they say, would call night. I found that if you really want to see darkness you have to drink three or four beers just before going to bed at around eleven o'clock. When you get up to pee about one, it's as dark as it gets, but not so dark you can't find the toilet in a strange cabin. That's important, since by then the generator has been turned off and the lights don't work.

Most days we spent two or three hours flying over genuinely trackless country, often at altitudes of two hundred feet or less, which is low enough to see bears, moose, caribou and even tundra swans clearly, not to mention stream after stream running red from spawning sockeye salmon. I must have asked a dozen people why the salmon turn red in the rivers, and the only one who knew was a native guy. "It's so the bears can see 'em," he said.

We often had the rivers we'd chosen entirely to ourselves, and that sense of loneliness was enhanced by the knowledge that now and then the plane doesn't show up to take you back to the nice, cozy lodge. This doesn't happen often (it never happened to us) but there *is* weather to consider, or engine trouble, and every now and then a pilot will get sick or even just forget he was supposed to pick you up, only to slap his forehead in a bar two days later, turn to the guy on the next stool and say, "Oh, shit." Fishermen are seldom lost forever, but they've been known to get stranded for a while.

At the time it seemed like an outrageous odyssey, but back

in Anchorage I found that we'd only gone a couple of inches down the Alaska Peninsula on a map of the state that would cover the average kitchen table. I went out on the front porch and tried to extrapolate the feeling of vastness from our own little trip to all the rest of that game- and fish-infested, largely roadless open land as an exercise in meditation. I sat there through two cans of beer and couldn't do it, but I did remember something Wallace Stegner had said on an audiotape DeWitt's company produced: something about how you don't even have to go into the wilderness to get its benefits; just knowing it's out there is a great comfort.

When we boarded the Alaska Airlines flight from Anchorage to Iliamna, the stewardess got on the intercom and said, "Fasten your seat belts and, yes, the reds are running." That was welcome news because I was psyched to catch salmon, as was everyone else on the plane. There were sixty-some passengers and exactly that many rod cases. No briefcases, no lap-top computers. We were there in late July so any salmon caught would probably be sockeyes, aka "reds." These are a marginal fly rod fish, many people said, but that hardly mattered.

For one thing, I'd spent a week fishing for Atlantic salmon in Scotland that same summer and had gotten skunked. I wasn't exactly looking for revenge—although going after, but not catching, a certain kind of fish does give you a long-lasting itch—there was just the idea of those millions of big fish that live somewhere out at sea and then run up into the rivers once a year, past orcas and seals and bears, to spawn and then die. When you come from a place where there are fewer fish and they pretty much stay put, that's romantic stuff.

And then there was the book tour I'd just finished. It was a mercifully short one, three cities in three days, but it was hell nonetheless. I'd be up too early to get breakfast, and with only one or two cups of coffee under my belt I'd be talking to a motor-mouth morning disc jockey who'd never fished and didn't seem to have read the book.

Then it was more or less constant media for the next six or seven hours. I'd appear on the noontime television talk show as a five-minute segment right after how to buy the perfect gift and just before household tips from kids. The interviewer had fished once as a kid, but he also didn't seem to have read the book. He'd read the press release, though.

"It says here that you're 'the undisputed bard of fly-fishing.' "

After a pause that's too long for television I said, "Yeah, I read that, too."

Despite my anarchistic tendencies, I was intimidated, so I lacked the courage to say, "Look, it's just some bullshit cooked up by the publisher, okay?" Back home some friends had started calling me the undisputed bard of fly-fishing, and then laughing hysterically.

Then came the reading/book signing. It's July in the Northwest, so it's warm and humid anyway. Then I get up on the podium in this stuffy room and they turn a battery of lights on me. These are the same lights they use to keep hamburgers hot in fast-food restaurants.

I'm thinking, If I'm gonna suffer this much, maybe I should get into something that really pays. I'm also thinking, In another fourteen hours I'll be in Alaska where I will burn this sport coat on DeWitt's front lawn. There are shuffling noises coming from the small crowd because I'm thinking instead of talking.

I got into salmon on our first day on the water. I was a little short on sleep and felt jet-lagged, even though I'd only crossed one time zone between Seattle and Anchorage. I guess it was the flying. I'm not as terrified of flying as I once was because I do more of it now. Then again, I can't shake the feeling that every time I fly and live I've used up a bit more luck.

We'd flown into the mouth of the Tazamina River and then motored upstream a mile or so. The water was full of sockeyes, but that didn't seem to interest anyone much except me. Dan, DeWitt and the guide were calmly speculating on where the rainbows and grayling might be, while I kept leaning over the gunnels saying, "Jesus Christ, look at all the salmon. Stop the god damn boat!" Most of the fish were nice and silvery, still fresh from the sea.

When we finally beached on a sand bar the guide got the other two guys going with streamers and then led me to a huge pod of sockeyes. He told me to rig a pink Polar Shrimp with split shot, as if I were fishing for trout with a nymph. One thing about the Alaskans: Unlike the Scots, they fish for salmon as if they actually want to catch them, with sink-tip lines and lead.

When the guide saw that I was rigging up an old Payne nine-and-a-half-foot light salmon rod with a brand-new Peerless #6 reel, he said he'd never seen one of those and asked to try it.

"Shoot," he said, "this is a little heavy, but it casts real nice."

There were fifty salmon in a pool not ten feet from where I was standing. "I'm glad you like the rod," I said, "but give it back."

I had a fish on for a minute or two and lost him. Then I got a good hookup, but the fish was snagged in the back. It weighed six or seven pounds and took longer to land than it should have.

I thought, Yeah, I've heard about this. There are those who say the plankton-eating sockeyes don't take flies and the best you can do is foul hook them, and there are others who say they do too take flies if you do it right. The rules say the fish is a keeper if it's hooked somewhere in the face, ahead of the gill covers.

If I remember right, I landed seven salmon that afternoon, four of which were hooked in or so close to the mouth that I'd say they either ate or tried to eat the fly. And that's as far as I care to delve into that controversy. I will say that when a sockeye is hooked near the front it fights real good, especially on a bamboo rod.

Those first few days we fished from the Iliaska Lodge, owned by Ted and Mary Gerkin. There's a long story here, and if you'd like to hear it you should read Ted's book, *Gamble at Iliamna,* because he tells it much better than I could. Anyway, it was here that I began to understand how sockeye salmon were viewed by Alaskan fly fishers.

The sockeyes, along with the kings, silvers, chums and pinks, form the basis for the entire ecology of these watersheds. The numbers of fish in these runs are astonishing: 6 million in this drainage, 19 million in that one, and there are hundreds of drainages.

Salmon often run all the way up into the smaller rivers and creeks, many of which are connected by large lakes. There are resident grayling and some Dolly Vardens in these streams, but the big rainbow trout and arctic char are only in the flowing water in significant numbers when they follow the salmon runs up out of the lakes. Sometimes a fisherman will say that Such-and-Such River isn't good for big rainbows yet because the salmon aren't in. If you're new at this you'll have to ask him what the hell he's talking about.

The trout, char and grayling feed on salmon eggs that are dribbled by the ripe hen salmon as they run up the rivers and then later on the ones that wash out of the spawning redds. This sounds like an incidental dietary footnote until you multiply the salmon by millions and get tons of protein from stray eggs alone.

The fish are really onto these things. It's said that big rainbows will swim over and nudge ripe hen salmon to dislodge eggs. Every guide and bush pilot I talked to claims to have seen that.

Still later, after the spawn when the salmon all die, these same game fish feed on bits of rotted salmon meat dislodged by the current. It's hard to picture, but in this scheme the pretty rainbow trout, char and grayling fall into the same ecological niche as maggots and vultures.

The standard flies are salmon egg patterns and sickly beige-colored "flesh flies," tied from rabbit fur. Naturally, these are fished on a dead drift. This may not be what you'd call classy stuff, but it does match the hatch perfectly.

The dying and dead salmon are also eaten by gulls, ravens, eagles, otters and such, not to mention aquatic insects, which then go on to feed the salmon parr and smolts before they return to the sea, as well as the grayling, trout, char and such during those times when there are no salmon in the rivers. Then the young salmon themselves form part of the diet for other game fish. In the middle of all this, you can go to the places where rivers enter lakes and fish streamers for big char collected there to feed on migrating smolts. The schools of char are often under flocks of excited, hungry gulls and terns.

That's the obvious stuff you can see from a boat or while wading a river. There's also the plankton/salmon/seal/orca connection out at sea. In the grand scheme, that's what salmon do: They bring the nutrients from the ocean far up into the freshwater rivers, lakes and streams and there's no way I can convey the magnitude of it. It's just something you have to see.

And then there are the bears. Alaskan brown bears—along with rainbow trout—put on a large part of every year's growth gorging on salmon, and once you've stepped in a huge, steaming pile of bear crap you begin to see that their droppings are not an insignificant contribution to the fertilizer needed to grow the grasses that are fed upon by the caribou that are now and then eaten by the bears—and so on.

This is efficient, economical, messy, smelly, mystically circular and temperamental. It's especially temperamental if you count the commercial netting of salmon—the "nylon curtain," they call it—that can screw things up seriously when it's not properly regulated, as most people will tell you it, in fact, is not. Take away the salmon, as some would gladly do for a single year's profit, and the ecosystem would die.

They say that the silvers and, in some circumstances, the kings are the real fly rod salmon in Alaska. The sockeyes are loved as a food fish and for their overall contribution to the food chain, but in the circles we were traveling in—fly fishers and fly-fishing guides—they don't seem to be too highly rated.

One morning at Iliaska when the weather was too socked in for flying, some of the guides drove a crew of us over to the Newhalen River to join seventy-five or so other fishermen who were dredging for sockeyes. This is called "combat zone fishing," and one of the guides told me the Newhalen was nothing. "You should see the rivers you can drive to from Anchorage," he said.

I got into it after a while, even though I claim not to like fishing in a crowd or chunking lead. I mean, what the hell; these were big fish and this was Alaska, where things are sometimes done differently. In the true spirit of things, I got deeply interested in killing some fish to take home.

By the way, I believe that "chunking" is the proper, common term. It's onomatopoetic, coming from the distinctive "chunk" sound split shot makes when it hits the water.

When the ceiling lifted after a few hours, Ted and another pilot flew over to pick us up and take us to a secluded little river to catch big rainbow trout, possibly on dry flies. "You're about to go from the ridiculous to the sublime," Ted said.

Rainbows are what the guides and lodge owners brag about most—in terms of both numbers and size—and they're what many visiting fly fishers are looking for. After all, this is one of the few places on earth where, at the right time, with some skill, a little luck and maybe the right guide, you can bag your ten- or twelve- or (if the stories can be believed) even your fifteen-pound rainbow on a fly rod. The fish will be scavenging behind a run of salmon instead of sipping mayflies but, if you connect, it will be a by God, double-digit wallhanger.

Not far from Iliamna Lake by float plane, on a river the name of which I've been asked not to mention, I landed a six-pound rainbow on a dry fly. It was a nice fish, big enough to make the lodge book (volume III), in which, among other things, you can record for posterity any trout over four pounds caught on a dry fly.

It was a nice fish, but not a great one by Alaskan standards; memorable only because it was hooked on a floating caddis pattern instead of on a sunken salmon egg, flesh fly or streamer. On the other hand, it was probably the biggest trout I've ever caught on a dry fly.

People have written pages in that lodge book about a single, good fish—eloquent stories filled with keen observations and humor—but I couldn't think of anything more profound than, "Six-pound rainbow on a #14 olive Stimulator," dated and signed. It's not that I wasn't happy, I was just a little tongue-tied.

We caught salmon on wet flies and split shot, nice-sized arctic char on eggs and Woolly Bugger streamers, rainbows on streamers and eggs, and one day I got into some pretty Dolly Vardens, once again on eggs. Apparently you don't do a lot of dry fly fishing in Alaska and I understand some fishermen on their first trip there are a little disillusioned by that.

I won't say I was actually disappointed, but there were a few times when I got enough of lead and sink-tips and flies that looked less like bugs or fish and more like bangles from a stripper's costume. And, yes, those did happen to be the few times when we weren't catching fish. I've noticed that certain fishing tactics seem a lot more acceptable when they're working.

Still, that day on the river Ted Gerkin asked me not to write about—the one where the big rainbows would come up to a dry caddis fly—was a tremendous relief, and so was our first afternoon at Wood River Lodge on the Agulawok River.

There were fish rising right in front of the cabin as we lugged our gear from the plane, and when we rushed down there we found that they were rainbows and grayling, both up to eighteen or twenty inches, rising to a this-and-that hatch of caddis, mayflies and small stoneflies. The fish weren't *too* picky, but we did have to fish flies that at least approximated the appearance of the real bugs. I was already in the water with my five-weight rod strung up, DeWitt was playing a fish and Dan had just missed a strike, when I learned that I had to run back to the cabin and dig my dry fly boxes out of the bottom of the duffel bag. At that point in the trip I had caught countless big fish, but it almost killed me that, for five minutes, Dan and DeWitt were getting them while I was looking for those damned fly boxes.

The next day we could have flown out once again to catch great big something-or-others someplace else, but we unanimously voted to stay and fish the river right in front of the lodge. They gave us two guides with boats, and we fished from right after breakfast—say, 8:00 in the morning—until dusk, which would have been going on midnight. Sure, we broke for a shore lunch and dinner at the lodge, but that's still a long day. In fact, this has happened to me at least once every time I've gone north. I say, "Jeeze, I'm kind of tired for some reason," and the bright-eyed guide says, "Well, we *have* been fishing for about sixteen hours now . . ."

We caught rainbows, some nice big arctic char and my biggest sockeye of the trip (ten pounds) on streamers, but what I remember most clearly now are the grayling.

They were almost all good-sized, maybe fifteen to twenty inches, and throughout the day we'd find pods of them rising in the slack water beside faster currents. "That's because they're a lazy fish," Duncan said. That's Duncan Oswald, one of several guides at Wood River who specialize in fly fishing. He also ties the flies for the lodge and knows the river's hatches. That's significant because in Alaska you don't *have* to know the hatches to catch fish.

I fished for the grayling with a seven-foot, nine-inch Mike Clark bamboo rod and Dan broke out a sweet little Pezon & Michelle Parabolic. Neither rod raised any eyebrows and, in fact, I was surprised at how many cane rods I saw on that trip. Apparently, many Alaskan fly fishers have a darling little bamboo stashed away for just these kinds of occasions.

As I said, the hatches were scattered, but the best was a fall of size fourteen dark stoneflies. The grayling would execute a refusal rise to a #14 Royal Wulff, *sometimes* eat an Elk Hair Caddis, Irresistible or Stimulator, and absolutely hammer an elegantly simple deer hair and calf tail stonefly of Duncan's own design. I brought a few of these home with me to copy.

Some people will tell you that grayling are an easy fish—the bluegills of the north—but I've never found them to be like that. The few times I've fished for them in their native range, they've been catchable, but far from pushovers: easy enough that you can usually get some, but still hard enough that each fish is an event. And, of course, they're unbelievably, iridescently beautiful. The perfect game fish, in other words.

That night at the lodge over gin and tonics, one of the other guides said it was too bad we hadn't gone off with him to catch the pigs but, more for Duncan's benefit than ours, I think, he said he did realize that a salmon egg is "chunked," while a dry fly is *"presented."*

I'm sorry to say I don't remember that guide's name now. We met so many guides and bush pilots I don't remember half their names, and I don't have them written down anywhere. Since I claim to be a professional writer, I should probably keep better notes but, looking back on previous trips, I sometimes think I've missed what could have been pure moments because I was busy scribbling in a damned notebook, making sure I'd be able to spell the name of the river when I got back home.

Of the pilots, a man with Branch River Air Service was the most overtly professional. Before takeoff, shouting over the racket of the engine, he told us how the doors opened and the location of the life vests and first aid kit. There was even an abbreviated version of the notorious seat-back safety card: a silhouette of the plane with arrows pointing to each side labeled "door."

That was the first time we flew with him. The next morning he said, "All the safety stuff is the same as it was yesterday, okay?"

Then there was the guy flying for Iliaska who could give you a quick, appraising glance and guess your weight within a few pounds, and then do the same with your gear. Payload weights are constantly on the minds of bush pilots.

John, with Wood River Lodge, was the most acrobatic flier. Usually if you pointed out wildlife while in a plane, everyone would look and nod approvingly, but John would shout, "Yeah, cool!" and go into a diving spin to get a closer look. The first time he did that it took me by surprise. I was squashed down in the seat and my cheeks felt heavy from the increased gravity of the spin. The ground was wheeling directly off my right shoulder and coming up fast. John asked, "Anyone here get airsick?" I said, "Not until now," but I don't think he could hear me over the roaring of the engine.

Bernie had the crazy bush pilot act down pat. He turned the engine over and yelled, "Jeeze, it started!" Then he looked down at his instruments and said, loudly but apparently to himself, "Hell, I guess all these little switches are in the right place." Then, turning to me in the copilot's seat, he asked, "You ever fly one of these?"

Once in the air he launched into a fishing story. The motor was howling. We were both wearing headphones, but all I could hear through mine was static, which is kind of what Bernie's voice sounds like anyway. I could see his lips moving. He made casting motions with his right hand, line stripping motions with his left and then held his palms up in front of him to indicate a fish (salmon? rainbow?) about three feet long.

I shouted "Far out" into my microphone, which is all you ever have to say to a fish story.

Bernie yells on the ground, too, as do many Alaskans. It's a survival tactic. A ranger at Katmai National Park told me about a park employee who had recently been mauled by a bear. "She's a very quiet person," the ranger said. This wasn't an idle comment on the victim's personality; he meant she wasn't talking loudly and constantly to herself as she walked through the woods, so she had come upon the bear unannounced. Bears don't like that.

We saw lots of bears in Alaska. They were following the salmon runs, as we were—inadvertently or otherwise—so it was unavoidable. These animals are called Alaskan brown bears, although there's some disagreement among the scientists about whether they're a separate species from the grizzly. The main difference is size. A big brown bear looks just like a grizzly, but stands a foot taller and weighs as much as six hundred pounds more. When you're sharing a gravel bar with one, size does seem to be a defining factor.

A big sow and a yearling cub came down to the Newhalen River the first day we fished it. I was about fourth in the line of fishermen upstream from the spot the bears wanted. When one of the guides hooted, "Bear!" I looked, broke off the eight-pound salmon I was playing without a second thought and began wading slowly but deliberately upstream, as they tell you to do. Dan, who doesn't like bears much, was just ahead of me. He didn't say anything, but he was making a quiet noise deep in his throat that sounded like the cooing of a pigeon.

Later, DeWitt said it was interesting to see the "ripple of recognition" go through us when the bears waded out into the river.

We saw bears almost every day, and there are three things people tell you about them: that, nine times out of ten, the bear will decline a confrontation; that if he *doesn't* decline, it's probably your fault; and that a bear's personal space is no less than fifty yards. That seemed awfully close. I found that I had to be at about two hundred before it would occur to me that the adults were handsome and the cubs were actually pretty cute. Bears scare me badly, but I still like them a lot, which I take as evidence that I've negotiated something heavy.

We only had two bear encounters that seemed ticklish. One day we flew into the Morraine River, a beautiful but bleak tundra stream known for big rainbows. We were dropped off at a small lake with our guide and the light inflatable raft we'd use to float a few miles of river down to the pickup point.

It was an unsettled day with gray, scudding clouds and winds between thirty and forty knots. The last thing the pilot said was that the weather would "probably" allow him to pick us up that evening. To understand Alaskan weather, all you have to do is look at one of the weather maps they sell in souvenir shops up there where various parts of the state are labeled partly shitty, mostly shitty, moderately shitty and so on.

Of course the wind made for grueling fly-casting, but we were still picking up a few big rainbows on Woolly Buggers and a thing I think they were calling an Electric Egg Sucking Leech, although I might not be remembering that correctly.

We'd stopped for lunch on a little stretch of sandy beach and the guide was talking to me about some other writers he'd guided. "They all wanted something for nothing," he said. "They expected to spend a day with me and come home with all the secrets I've learned in ten years in the bush." I was just beginning to explain that all I wanted to know was what fly to tie on when a bear popped out of the brush about forty yards away.

He stood up on his hind feet and squinted at us. Bears

don't see well, but he knew there was something on this sand bar that wasn't there the last time he'd looked. The wind was blowing hard at right angles between us and the bear, so he couldn't get our scent.

When the bear dropped to all fours and came a little closer—cautious, but seized by curiosity—I asked the guide, "Should we launch the raft?" He said, "What good would that do?" and I remembered what someone had said a few days before: "You think you're safe in a boat until you see one of those guys trot across a deep, fast stream as if it wasn't even there." The Morraine was a small river, swift and deep here and there, but wadable by humans in most places.

Then the bear walked into the underbrush and we lost sight of him. Dan asked, "What should we do now?" and the guide said, "Finish your lunch."

Another day we flew into a spot where a small creek entered a lake. The plan was to wade up the creek a half mile or so to a place where, we'd been assured, there were huge rainbows and grayling, but there was a sow and two cubs around the first bend, so we had to turn back and work the inlet, where there didn't seem to be too many fish.

I won't try to describe the whole, grim dance in detail, but eventually a young male bear came down to the inlet and made it known that we had blundered into his personal space and that he wasn't pleased. Since he was on shore and we were already up to our armpits in the lake, we had a little trouble getting out of his way, although we tried. At one point the bear gave us some negative body language—lowered head, flattened ears. This doesn't sound like much on paper, but on site it's pretty damned impressive.

That bear herded us back and forth across the inlet a few times, and at one point Dan and DeWitt both lost their footing and went under while trying to move a little more deliberately than was possible in deep water and slippery rocks. At that point I was closest to the bear—I can't say how close, but far less than the prescribed fifty yards—and I kept my footing not because I'd remained calm exactly, but because I'd already come to terms with a horrible death and was wondering how badly I'd be missed back home.

Throughout the whole thing our guide, Nanci Morris, spoke in a calming voice, first to the bear, then to us, and she never unholstered her Smith and Wesson .44 magnum. She was the picture of composure, and said later she was more worried about that sow getting nervous because boars are known to attack cubs.

It turned out okay, but I was glad to hear the deep, unmistakable drone of the DeHavilland Beaver Nanci calls the Cream Puff coming to pick us up. It occurred to me that having an airplane come and save you from a bear is a great way to get over your fear of flying. When the plane taxied in, Dan waded out and kissed a pontoon, able to kid around now because it seemed we'd live.

Nanci is the head guide (excuse me, "Director of Sportfishing") at the Quinnat Landing Hotel in the town of King Salmon. Her specialty is trophy-sized kings, and in some magazine article or brochure she was once dubbed "the queen of the king salmon guides." Naturally, that stuck, as embarrassing publicity always does.

When I said something about getting to be head guide at a place like that at an obviously tender age, Nanci said, "Yeah, and, not to put too fine a point on it, try doing it as a woman."

I could see that. Competence is admired in a place like King Salmon, but men far outnumber women and at times the horniness is almost palpable. And it's a little rough—in a pleasant way for a tourist, but rough nonetheless. Over some beers in the hotel bar a pilot named Red told me, "We try to make a year's living here in five or six months, so we fight sleep deprivation half the year and depression the other half." He also said, gazing wistfully out at the Naknik River,

"Ah, Alaska. She seduces you every summer and then abandons you every winter."

Anyway, Nanci does seem to love that plane with something close to a passion. As head guide, she almost always manages to schedule it for her own trips and, although she talked about other things in the two days we all spent together, she kept coming back to the Cream Puff. When we walked down to the dock to board it or when it banked in to land and pick us up, she'd say, "Just look at it. God!"

It *is* a sweetheart. You see all kinds of other aircraft, but the Beaver is the classic, workhorse bush plane, the one everyone wants. They were discontinued in the 1960s, but they're still widely in use because, like only a handful of other things in life, they are absolutely perfect as is. This one is painted deep purple with a silver lightning bolt down each side, and it's a "cherry rebuild"—might as well be brand new. A plane is everything in Alaska, and a great plane is sublime.

The first time I saw the Cream Puff it was sitting at a dock on the Naknik River and we were sitting in the bar at Quinnat Landing, near the big picture windows, eating thick steaks and talking about the fishing. During a lull in the conversation, Nanci gazed out at the Beaver and said, "See that plane out there? I love that plane. If that plane was a man, I just might say 'I do.' "

At which point every man in the joint looked out the window at the lovely old purple Beaver. Its big radial engine was idling. At that range it sounded like the purring of a large, happy cat.

13

Tying

GINGER QUILL

*E*very winter—usually sometime in January—I resolve to tie flies two or three nights a week so that, by spring, all my fly boxes will be neat and well-stocked, like assault rifles with full clips, like sports cars with well-tuned engines, like . . . well, there's no good analogy. Like fly boxes stuffed with fresh, neat flies—enough to catch a thousand fish. Then, every spring, I realize I only made a medium-sized dent and I'm a little disappointed in myself.

Maybe I should stop doing that. In fact, I read somewhere that traditional New Year's–style resolutions are going out of style because we Americans are getting either lazier or more realistic.

I wouldn't feel so bad if I'd spent the time rereading the great books I didn't fully appreciate in college, but the fact is I can't remember what happened to most of those long, cold nights except that I didn't tie flies. And that, I hate to admit, suggests an unhealthy amount of television.

But I do get the flies tied—usually in frantic sessions before trips, sometimes actually *on* those trips—and that's not all bad. Tying Green Drakes for an expedition that starts in two days, or whipping out some Pale Morning Duns on the tailgate of a pickup for a hatch that begins in an hour, adds a kind of immediacy to the job that I've come to like. And if the tailgate flies aren't exactly flawless, they still catch fish as often as not, which puts things into perspective.

Some fishermen actually prefer to tie their flies that way— through the season, as needed—but I liked it the few times I had at least the standard patterns pretty well-stocked. If nothing else, it kept that short notice tying time free. After all, you never know what's going to come up.

For example, around here some of the best mayfly hatches are the Blue-winged Olives. There are two sizes of fly—eighteens and twenty-twos—and they come off more or less predictably twice a year, spring and fall. To most of us these bugs are old, predictable friends, so we carry a variety of fly patterns to copy the nymphs, emergers and duns. We tend to neglect the spinners, though, because they're usually not "important," as they say.

But then last fall, for reasons I won't even guess at, the spinners (the adult, mating stage of these bugs) were at least as important as the more recognizable duns.

The trout did feed on the emerging duns, but the usually long, luxurious hatches tended to be sparse and short that season, and they were coming earlier in the day, too. Then the spinner falls would come on in late afternoon, especially on overcast days, and the bugs would be on the water for hours, with trout sipping them lazily and steadily. Often the spinners of both species would be on the water at the same time and the trout, in their typical, perverse way, always seemed to want the smaller one.

The first day A.K. and I hit this I did have a few tiny spinners in my fly box. They were old ones that I hadn't used in a long time, but I'd tied them because every now and then a dun hatch would be followed in the early evening by a light spinner fall, or early in the morning, before the hatch, you could find the odd fish rising in a backwater to a few leftover spinners from the night before. It was one of those flies that might get you into a few extra fish but that was not crucial to a good day's fishing. Many fishermen here don't carry any Blue-winged Olive spinners at all, and claim they don't miss them.

On that first day there was a smattering of large and small olive duns in the late morning, then a long lull, and then a glorious, blanket spinner fall in the afternoon. At first we didn't know what it was. Fish were rising all over the place in the glassy currents at the backs of the pools, and we thought it must be a midge hatch because of the casual porpoising way they were feeding. When we waded in and saw all the spinners on the water, we knew what they had to be, but it still took a minute to sink in. A.K. and I have fished Blue-winged Olive hatches together for a couple of decades now, and in all that time I don't think either of us had ever seen a full-blown spinner fall.

The #18 spinner (the one I had a few copies of) was a rusty red color, and the little #22, what we're told is a Paraleptophlebia, was a pale olive. I landed a few trout using a #22 Trike spinner—the wrong color (black body instead of olive) but the right size. I only had two of them, though, and I soon lost them to fish. There were some big trout rising, and I was fishing the kind of long, fine tippet that gives you a good, lifelike drift, but breaks easily.

So I ended up using a #18 Rusty Spinner. A few trout liked it well enough to eat it, but most didn't, and the few that did were little ones. This was one of those days when A.K. seriously outfished me. Not that either of us was counting, you understand, but one does notice.

Then A.K. somehow got down there without me for a day. He called the next morning and said he'd absolutely hammered trout on a spinner fly pattern of his own design: size twenty-two, sparse dun tails, body of dyed olive quill, black dubbed thorax and white hackle tip wings. (Right. Obvious. I'd have thought of it myself eventually.) He wanted to go back to the river the next day, so I sat down and tied a dozen of the flies he'd described.

This was a straightforward pattern, but it still took me a few tries to get a feel for the size and proportions. I tied a dozen (a nice, round, professional-sounding number) and except for the first two they were all trim and pretty.

Then Ed called and said he was going to meet us there. I told him I had *the* fly pattern and he said, "Good, I may have to borrow some from you."

So I went back and tied another half dozen so as to avoid being placed in a position I've been in more than once before: The fish are biting, I have the right fly, but there are only two left. One of my oldest and dearest friends wades over and says, "Can I bum one of those from you?" and I'm forced to say, "Look, man, life is hard."

The fly itself is a lovely thing and, as simple as it is, it's a surprisingly good copy of the natural insect. The fish liked it. I'd tied enough that I could have loaned some to Ed, but it turned out that he'd stayed up late tying a bunch of his own. Ed's like me in this regard, he has nothing against catching trout on other people's flies, but it's just noticeably better if you tied them yourself.

That was last fall, as I said. At this writing, the spring Olive hatches haven't started yet, but I can almost guarantee that they'll come in the old familiar mode: good hatches of duns followed by obscure spinner falls that surely happen sometime, somewhere, but that you never actually see.

Still, if I ever do see it again, I'll have the pattern. Sure, the little Trike spinner would probably work just as well, but it wouldn't be *exactly* the right fly, so trout caught on it— though better than no fish at all—would also fall short of being perfect. In fact, that seems to be where half the flies in my boxes came from in the first place. They represent something that happened once, and so will surely happen again eventually, given enough time. In that way, my fly selection makes sense in the same way my life does, that is, only to me.

There are some tiers, both amateur and professional, who produce perfect flies, and sometimes those fly patterns are startlingly accurate, right down to, as Dave Whitlock once said, "eyeballs, elbows and arseholes."

It's flies like these—incredibly detailed, every hair and feather in place—that tempt some of us, in emotional moments, to call fly-tying an "art." But if it *is* art, it's an unusual medium.

To tie a Ginger Quill dry fly—a simple, standard pattern—you start with a high-quality, light wire hook; tie in a few fibers from a ginger-colored spade hackle, cocked slightly upward for a tail; wrap on a pair of stripped ginger hackle stems for a trim, segmented, subtly tapered body; tie in a pair of dun-colored hen hackle tips for wings, with careful thread wraps between them so they're separated at the proper angle; wrap on a long ginger hackle so that the hackle collar extends just past the gap of the hook; wrap a small, neat head of tying thread and finish it off with a drop of clear lacquer.

It's a lovely fly that you'll admire for a few seconds before you drop it into your box and go on to the next one. Then, as soon as possible, you'll throw it in a river and let a bunch of trout chew on it until it comes apart or breaks off.

It's a matter of perception and presentation. If you put a frame around it, it's art; if you use it, it's craft. If you *could* use it but put a frame around it instead, I don't know what the hell it is.

True, flies by some famous tiers (especially dead ones)

can be worth a lot as collector's items, and you'll sometimes see exceptionally well-made trout and salmon flies mounted in shadow box frames. Still, a working fly, by its very nature, is a handsome but expendable item. So the second best thing you can say about a professional tier is that his flies are absolutely beautiful, but the *best* thing you can say is that they're just fine and he can tie two and a half dozen in an hour.

A.K. taught me most of what I know about fly-tying. It turned out to be a classic paradox—a simple job with endless complications—but the upshot is, tying flies is like splitting wood neatly or plowing a straight furrow: If there's an art to it, it's in the work itself rather than in the product.

I try to tie most of the flies I use myself, not as a matter of pride exactly, but just because there's a little more satisfaction to it. I do buy some occasionally, especially when there's some weird, regional pattern the local trout are insane for, and having tied professionally myself, I don't wince too much at the two dollars or so you can pay for a single fly now, even though I started tying my own when sixty-five cents apiece seemed too steep.

But of course money isn't the object. The object is to do as much of the work yourself as possible, thereby becoming self-sufficient and gaining the kind of nonlinear understanding that spreads in a circle around what seems, at first glance, to be the soul of the matter.

Eventually you may become like A.K., a professional tier who, except under the most dire circumstances and for reasons of his own, would rather not catch fish at all than catch them on someone else's flies.

Last summer A.K., Ed and I went to fish some private brook trout ponds not far from here. Ed had never fished the ponds before, so he called a few days early to ask what flies he needed to tie. "Small hoppers, damselfly nymphs and adult damsels," I said, because that's what the owner of the pond had told me.

We got on the water a little after noon on a warm, bright, breezy day—classic grasshopper weather. This little pond is set in an open foothills meadow that's covered with tall grass, and the few rises were all within a foot or two of the upwind bank, exactly where errant hoppers would be.

Yes, I know you're supposed to go into the scientific mode, check the water to see what bugs are there and then copy them, but sometimes it's too perfect, too obvious.

Ed and I tied on #14 hoppers because the owner had said to use small ones. A.K. didn't have any that size, so he tied on a big one, maybe a #8. "How much difference could it make?" he asked rhetorically.

I hooked a fish on my third or fourth cast, and by the time I'd released it, Ed had one on. They were both good brookies: maybe thirteen or fourteen inches, healthy, chunky and well-colored that far from spawning season.

We took a few more each along that east bank, and then we began to notice that A.K. wasn't getting them. We noticed this because it was quite odd. A.K. is an excellent fly fisher, and it's rare for him to be the one guy out of three who's not catching fish.

Of course you're not supposed to gloat at a time like that, but sometimes, in the glow of a few nice fish, your baser instincts get the best of you.

"I have a whole bunch of these little hoppers," I said to A.K. "I'd offer you one, but I know you refuse to fish with flies you didn't tie yourself."

"That's correct," he said.

It seemed as though the grasshopper action consisted of a handful of decent-sized brook trout working along that one bank. Ed and I either caught them all or we caught enough to spook the rest of them. We also found that they didn't care for the standard grasshopper twitch, they wanted the flies to lie absolutely still on the surface. Pretty picky for brook trout.

After the hopper fall was over, there was no clearly "right" fly pattern. We caught our fish on a variety of flies: damsel nymphs, floating beetles, the odd streamer, things like that. A.K. even made his big grasshopper work on one fish, which delighted him. Being a man of few words—at least while fishing—he held the trout up for us to see and said, "There!"

I've noticed that professional tiers, like artists, can sometimes get cranky. Or maybe it's the crankiness that comes first, giving them the predisposition to be meticulous and single-minded. For most of us, making our own flies is just a comfortable part of the process of fishing, a way to get inside of things in a nonscientific, somewhat intuitive and, okay, maybe even artistic way.

For the most part, fly-tying is a practical business. You want the flies to work, you want them to be as durable as the materials will allow, and you want to be able to tie them quickly and easily enough that you can use them up thoughtlessly.

Okay, fine, but then sooner or later the elements of style begin to creep in. You may begin to tie flies that are prettier than they'd have to be just to catch fish for reasons that aren't immediately evident. The bodies on your dry flies become trimmer, and not necessarily because trout like them better that way. There are hundreds of colors of commercial dubbing on the market, but none of them are quite right, so you begin to dye and blend your own. It's great when someone tells you you tie a pretty fly, but that's not precisely why you do it.

When you settle on one or two patterns to copy a bug you see often, you feel you've begun to gain some purchase on the hatch. Your Brown Drake is not just a brown *Green* Drake, because, although you can't put your finger on it, the former has quirks that the latter doesn't. There's a certain posture on the water, a way of holding the tail up a few extra degrees, maybe something you could only describe as the bug's attitude.

You feel as if you have some kind of understanding, and

catching a couple of fish seems like proof of that, so even on a strange river in a different state, you feel nicely at home.

There was a time when fly patterns were pretty much fixed and unassailable, but it's not like that anymore. Now it's perfectly okay if your patterns are a little different from anyone else's. Maybe it's even preferable, because the flies you tie are seen as a kind of self-expression.

Of course this isn't aimless. The practical end saves you from getting too self-indulgent and keeps you fundamentally engaged with the environment. As a fly tier, you can't get otherworldly because a beautiful fly that doesn't catch fish is *not* a beautiful fly. On the other hand, evaluating a fly solely on whether it catches fish is like saying a painting of Elvis on velvet is as good as a Picasso because both will cover the same crack in the plaster.

Not long ago I ran into a kid in West Yellowstone, Montana, who said he'd just come back from the Madison River. He was wearing a clean vest, new waders and a fluorescent orange hat. I'd say he was in his late teens or early twenties.

"How'd you do?" I asked.

"I caught my first trout on a fly I tied myself," the kid said proudly. This is a little like introducing a woman as your first wife: an admission that this is now, but more will surely happen.

I didn't ask how big the fish had been because that was clearly not the point, and I also stopped myself from putting a fatherly hand on his shoulder and saying something like, "You will remember this day for the rest of your life, my son," because some middle-aged guy pontificating wouldn't have added to the moment.

I said, "Congratulations," he said, "Thanks," and I walked over to my borrowed, bat-infested cabin to get some sleep. It was eleven o'clock and I'd been fishing all day myself.

And then it occurred to me that I didn't remember my first trout on my own fly. I stopped just outside the circle of the porch light and thought about it. The woods were dark. Off to the right I could hear the little spring creek gurgling.

It would have to have been sometime in the late 1960s. I'd guess it was a small brown trout from the St. Vrain River on an Adams dry fly, but that would only be a guess. I couldn't actually picture the fish, the river, the fly pattern or, oddly enough, even the feeling.

Oh, well, it must have really been something at the time.

14

A Few Days Before Christmas

A few days before Christmas last year, A.K. and I drove down to Pike National Forest and hiked into the Cheesman Canyon stretch of the South Platte River. The weather had been chilly for at least a week (meaning the water would be cold, even for trout), word was the flow was down to about thirty cubic feet per second (too low) and the grapevine hadn't had anything to say about the midge hatches in a while, which meant they were probably off. If there was any good news, it was that the river wasn't frozen bank to bank.

All the signs pointed to poor fishing or, as A.K. would say, in the tone of a schoolteacher correcting your grammar, "poor *catching*," since the fishing itself is always good. Now that I think about it, I guess that was the whole point.

I hadn't been out fishing—or doing much of anything else—in almost a month, and I was beginning to think all my friends were getting too old. All are at least in their forties now, and they seem so damn busy. No one had called to say, "Well, nothing much is happening, but let's at least go look at the Frying Pan River," or, "It's pretty cold, but let's see if we can shoot a couple of rabbits." When *I* made the calls, people were saying, "Oh, I don't know, this is happening, that's happening . . . I don't know . . ." God, I thought, I'm hanging out with a bunch of old men.

And for about that same month, A.K. had been back at his family home in Iowa. His father had died, and there were all those sad, final chores to be taken care of, including the selling of the farm where A.K. was born. In a typical example of understatement, he said it hadn't been much fun.

We talked about it a little when he got back, but I've noticed that in situations like this there's often surprisingly little to say. The late Mr. Best had lived a good, long, honest, largely uneventful life farming the land he was born on; hunting rabbits with the .22 rifle he'd bought used in the 1920s because it would have gone against his practical, Protestant upbringing to pay seven whole dollars for a new one. This kind of personal history is all but obsolete now and, aside from everything else, *that's* a damned shame.

I won't presume to speculate about what A.K. was feeling or what he had to "work through," as they say, but I knew he was not in a good mood. As for me, real trouble should show me that my own little problems are really nothing, but I'm more likely to see it as proof that a festering cloud of doom is settling on everything.

Anyway, when A.K. called and said he needed to go fishing, I said, "Yeah, I do, too," and I understood it wasn't going to matter much if the trout weren't biting.

• • •

We walked into the canyon at the fastest pace we could manage on the dangerously icy trail. On the drive down we had carefully established that there wasn't much chance of catching any fish, but once we were there a little of the old excitement began to kick in. We noted that there were no cars at the trailhead parking lot and no fresh tracks on the trail. That meant—for what it was worth—that we'd probably have the whole three miles of river to ourselves.

After looking at a few good pools, we settled on an old favorite spot. The day was chilly with a low, solid overcast and the water temperature on A.K.'s stream thermometer read thirty-six degrees, or four degrees below the trout's lower avoidance level. When the water temperature drops below forty, the trout become sluggish and so do the aquatic insects they feed on. It's a matter of predators evolving to match the habits of their prey, or at least that's how I like to see it.

And fishermen, bundled in three times the clothing they'd need for a hike on a cold day, can get a little sluggish themselves. You think of evolution because on a cold trout stream in midwinter, time seems numbingly huge. We stood there for a few minutes looking at the river. "This is going to be tough," I said, and A.K. replied, "Well, we knew that."

The fly to fish at a time like that is a String Thing. This is no more than a layer of white thread wrapped on a #20 hook, but it's almost an exact copy of the little wormlike midge larvae that are so numerous in that stretch of the Platte. Even on days when the food chain is turned down as low as it will go and the fish are sulking, you can sometimes get them to inhale a String Thing if you're persistent enough and your drifts are close to perfect.

This fly is so simple as to be offensive to A.K.—who's a professional fly tier, after all—but he sometimes has a few of them tucked into a corner of one of his fly boxes where maybe no one will notice them.

This is the kind of repetitive, meditational fishing that requires not so much skill as something I've heard called thoughtless, harmonious concentration. It's the kind of job that doesn't take all your wits; just enough of them to keep you from thinking very rigorously of anything else. On a cold day it also requires a twig fire and a pot of coffee on shore, which you repair to just *before* your feet actually go numb.

Wading out of the water to sit by the fire for a while is easy when the fishing is slow, and at those times the conversation wanders all over the place, from politics to fishing to sleeping bag design to the proper way to make boiled coffee. A.K. didn't say anything about his father that I can remember now, but, because it was in the air, I caught myself thinking about *my* dad a little when the talk petered out.

It occurred to me that I'm now a better fisherman than he was—maybe even a better outdoorsman in general—but that's only because I've had the time to put into it. I never did have the family or the regular job or his sense of "what a grown man's responsibilities in life ought to be." I still recall bits and pieces of the lectures, and I guess those memories aren't exactly fond ones.

Dad and I didn't see eye to eye about a lot of things, but that's only natural. When you grow up seeing one way in life, you're very likely to choose another for yourself, if only for some variety. But I think he'd have liked it that I moved out to Colorado where I fish a lot and make a decent living writing stories about it. He might even have come to understand why I didn't get all clobbered up with a lot of dependents and responsibilities. Dad liked to hunt and fish, but he never did as much of either as he'd have liked. He planned to make up for that after he retired, but he never made it that far. Many of the fathers of my generation did this same thing: They gave up what they thought of as childish things because they thought they were supposed to, and it killed a lot of them.

If Dad had lived, he might not have ended up sharing my

bohemian views on life, but when he saw that the result was a lot more fishing time, I'll bet he'd at least have stopped bitching at me.

So I didn't grow up to be my father (that's a kind of victory for most boys), but in some ways I may have become the man my father wanted to be, which is, I guess you'd say, interesting.

I did get one thing from him, though: the worst kind of workaholism. That's the kind where you're not always busy, but you always feel that you should be, so it can be hard to goof off effectively. One of the few times I can do nothing with a clear conscience is when I'm sitting next to a twig fire on the bank of a trout stream. And that, I suppose, is because nothing is all you can do when you're waiting for the fishing to pick up—even if it probably won't pick up for a month.

A.K. and I did well that day when you consider that, by rights, we shouldn't have caught anything at all. There was a period of less than an hour in midafternoon when the water temperature must have reached up into the low forties. I was fishing along on automatic pilot when a big trout bit my fly, bent the hook almost straight and got away before I could even think of giving it line. A few minutes later I hooked another one and got it almost to the net before it threw the hook. I really wanted to land that fish, but then when it got off I was glad I didn't have to freeze my hands releasing it. It was a nice rainbow. Maybe sixteen inches.

I switched to a little dry fly when I saw a single trout rise twice near the far bank, but by the time I got the knot tied the fish had stopped. I made a few casts anyway, notwithstanding the feeling that it was useless.

Fifty yards downstream, A.K. also had a few risers. He missed one and hooked and landed another on a dry fly. When he got that fish to the net, he gave a quiet little "whoop" so I'd notice. On a day when more fish were being caught, this wouldn't have been necessary.

After that the river went dead again and pretty much stayed that way until dark. We doused the fire and wandered around a little, doing more looking than fishing and making some tentative plans. In the coming year, aside from the fishing we'd naturally do around Colorado, there was the possibility of bass in Texas, trout in Montana, various game fish in Alaska and Atlantic salmon on a river somewhere in Canada.

Well, maybe these were just ideas instead of plans, but there comes a time when the former has to be bravely turned into the latter. Otherwise, you just talk and think and eventually they dissolve, either because other things pile up or because it just gets to be too late to do anything about them.

And there's another wrinkle to all this. The possible Alaska trip had to do with some friends who were moving there soon and who had already invited several of us to come up. "As soon as we get a line on something" (meaning good fishing), "we'll let you know," they said.

These folks are good planners, but they're also enthusiastic and quick to seize the moment. It wouldn't surprise me to get a phone call from them saying, "Be here in a week, the something-or-others are running."

This involves a fine point in the art of planning: maintaining the mental balance and self-confidence it takes to let you go at a moment's notice. Ed told me once that when he was younger he'd automatically say "yes" when some frantic fisherman called with little more than a rumor, while now he sees this creeping tendency to say "no" just as compulsively.

"It's something you need to pay attention to," he said, and I agree. Half of getting old is inexorable biology, but the other half is attitude.

My father liked to have things planned out in detail and I see that tendency in myself, but I've also learned to like the idea that I really don't know what's going to happen. I might as well like it because that's the way it is.

Ed again: "If you knew exactly what was gonna happen on a trip, you wouldn't even have to go."

So A.K. and I wandered the river like this, strolling, talking, making a few halfhearted casts here and there. The day had stayed that same, uniform damp gray, with the rock cliffs and the sky both looking like the undersides of old iron ships. If it had been warmer, it would have been great fishing weather.

We saw two ravens perched in a dead ponderosa pine tree. Every now and then one of them would turn to the other and poke it hard with its beak a few times. The bird getting poked didn't seem to respond in any way. I'm only an amateur bird watcher, which means I know what a raven is, but I have no idea why one would poke his partner like that.

There might have been another short flurry of feeding activity from the trout, but it was unlikely. It seemed as if it had gotten colder, although it may have only felt that way because we'd been out in it for so long. I do carry a little thermometer/compass gadget on my day pack, but I've found that I don't need an instrument to tell me when I'm cold.

We didn't stay until the light was almost gone out of desperation for more trout, but simply because that's what one does, probably in part because both our dads had that linear view of things. We're here to fish, so we fish. A equals B, period.

So in one way we were were just going through the motions. On the other hand, we ended up at a pool called the Ice Box because that was the most likely place to find feeding trout late on a cold December afternoon. You stay the whole day as a kind of observance, but you don't entirely blow off the fishing either.

On the way down to that last pool we had to cross a little

rip in the current, and A.K. pulled out ahead. He's thirteen years my senior, but he still wades better than I do in fast water, although both of us have gotten a little more careful in recent years. It's funny, but I didn't notice that a little of the spring had gone out of his step until it was back.

CHAPTER

15

The Fishing Contest

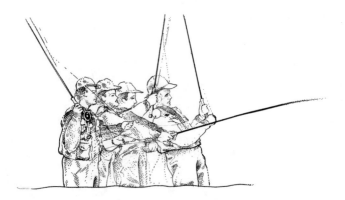

*I*n September of 1991 I took part in the first annual Colorado Fly-casting Open tournament, a two-day event that was held in and around Lyons, Colorado. This was my first and only venture into competitive fishing, unless you count those arrangements where, for instance, the guy who catches the smallest fish of the day has to buy the beer.

I was talked into it. Bamboo rodmaker Mike Clark, an old friend of mine, was one of the organizers, and since this was a new and largely unknown event, they were trying to drum up contestants.

I walked into Mike's shop one afternoon to bum a cup of coffee and he said, "You're gonna fish in the tournament, aren't you?" I'd known this was coming, but I'd tried not to think about it. I guess I'd secretly hoped that if I just didn't volunteer it would slide by.

At first I said I disapproved of competitive fishing on philosophical grounds—the same terse answer I'd given the two or three other times I'd been asked to get into an official fishing contest of some kind. That had worked in the past and it was still true, but this time it sounded awfully self-righteous—the kind of crap you can sometimes lay on strangers, but not on friends. After all, who am I to approve or disapprove of anything?

"I don't mean to say it's the devil's work," I added, "I just don't think I'd like it."

"You ever do it?" Mike asked.

"No."

"So how do you know you wouldn't like it?"

My mother used to get me with that one.

I began to soften a little then. As I said, this was the first time this thing had ever been held, and there did seem to be some decent arguments for it: "It'll help build a constituency for conservation work on the stream," one guy said, and someone else pointed out that it could illustrate to the chamber of commerce types that a proper local industry is one that recognizes the value of a healthy natural environment. You know, fly-fishing instead of a paper mill.

And, too, I think the people behind the event—some friends of mine among them—were beginning to ask that inevitable question: What if we had a contest and nobody entered?

"How much is the entry fee?" I asked.

"A hundred dollars."

"Forget it," I said.

Mike glanced out through his shop window at the one-block, one-story main street and said, "Tell you what. I'll sponsor you."

"Oh, hell . . ."

Fly-fishing contests aren't exactly sweeping the country, thank God, but they have gotten more popular in the last few years. The one everybody knows about is the Jackson Hole One Fly in Jackson Hole, Wyoming. Jack Dennis started this in the mid-eighties and, by most accounts, he's the one who invented the idea of contestants being limited to one fly for the whole event.

All the other fly-fishing contests I've heard of mimic this one pretty closely. Teams or individuals fish for a day—accompanied by guides, sometimes called "judges"—and the score is figured on either total trout or total *inches* of trout fairly landed. When there are teams, sometimes the individual who catches the biggest or the most fish gets a little something extra. I've never heard of the species of trout affecting the scoring, but I understand that in the Colorado Superfly Competition Kokanee salmon are somehow scored differently.

Often specific beats on the river are assigned by drawing, and they're usually rotated between morning and afternoon sessions so no one can complain that the other team got the honey hole.

And there's always that thing with the flies. You get one or sometimes two flies, picked by you beforehand and then approved by the judges, and that's it. Lose it (or them) and you're done.

That naturally adds some artificial tactical aspects to it. You fish more carefully than you normally would, passing up good but tricky flies, and you use a cable of a leader that ruins your drifts. And of course a bad choice of fly pattern can't be corrected, so you pick a general attractor-style fly and then hope against a hatch instead of for one.

The choice of fly can be agonizing. There are those who'll fish a nymph in competition because, on a normal day on a normal trout stream, more fish can be caught on nymphs than on dry flies. Then there are those who'll fish a dry fly because you're less likely to lose it and because, in a pinch, it's easier to sink a dry fly than float a nymph.

You want a durable fly that won't fall apart with hard use. The rules of some contests let you fix a fly on-stream, but no actual fly-tying materials can be used. Repairs must be done with monofilament or "natural material commonly found on the stream." That would be grass and strips of tree bark rather than aluminum cans and plastic bags. I'm told that's usually a losing battle, so many fishermen tie up indestructible tournament flies using heavy thread, extra knots, wire and Super Glue.

Virtually all of these events are held for charity or, if you're like me and don't care for that word, let's say the proceeds go to fund a good, usually conservation-related cause.

The come-ons for these things usually talk about how much media exposure they'll get, as if media exposure in and of itself was a good thing, and about what the money that's raised will go for. Sometimes it's something specific, like habitat improvement on this or that stream, although sometimes it goes into some vague pot labeled "preservation of cold water fisheries," which could mean anything. A fair question to ask of any apparently good cause is, "How much of the money *actually goes to feed starving children in South America?*" or whatever.

Prizes are seldom if ever cash. Usually the top fisherman gets something like a good fly rod, maybe a little loving cup of the "World's Greatest Dad" variety for the mantel and the opportunity to bask briefly in whatever media glitz there might be. In other words, the prize is worth winning, but nowhere near enough to cheat for, which tends to keep things pretty laid back.

That's a saving grace. If anyone thinks we need a snazzier fly-fishing tournament with more industry sponsors and a bigger purse, all he should have to do is look at the horrors of competitive bass fishing: Top four anglers compete for seventy thousand dollars cash. And it's held at Disney World! And it's broadcast on The Nashville Network. That's not fishing, that's the kind of thing that has made the sports pages of most newspapers read like a cross between the business section and the police notes.

Jack Dennis's One Fly is still the undisputed big one in fly-fishing, and with luck it's as big as these things will ever get. It attracts celebrities and I'm told it's quite the scene, although there have been no scandals that I know of and I've yet to see a razzle-dazzle press release crowing about crowds and prize money both in the hundreds of thousands. I've talked to some people who have fished in the One Fly and they claim they actually had fun.

There can be as many as thirty-two four-person teams in the One Fly, plus guides, and it's popular enough that in recent years it's been by invitation only. There are several formal dinners involved and the entry fee is three thousand dollars per team. But from what I've seen of them, most of the fly-fishing tournaments are still small, local, funky, friendly and comparatively cheap to enter. The printed rules tend to be detailed, but brief and light on the legalese, except, of course, for the liability waiver.

The first Colorado Open was small and friendly enough and maybe even a little funkier than it was intended to be, but it was different from most in two ways. For one thing, it was for profit. Sure, there was an implication that the town of Lyons might well use the proceeds for stream improvement or research into minimum flows, but there were no promises. For another, at least part of it was an old-style *casting* tournament with courses for distance and accuracy based largely on the rules of the American Casting Association in Fenton, Missouri.

According to the organizers, the Colorado Open was designed to be a test of all-around fly-fishing skill under conditions that, as much as possible, resemble those of actual fishing. I wasn't on the planning committee, but I lobbied some people who were to bag the fishing event entirely and just make it a casting tournament. I said that the distance and accuracy courses might be a fair way to pick the best caster, but that one random day of fishing with only two flies wasn't a fair test of a fisherman's ability to catch trout. And anyway, fly-fishing, by nature, is a sport that doesn't—or shouldn't—involve rivalry. I quoted Jim Harrison: "Any spirit of competition in hunting or fishing dishonors the game," he said.

Someone asked, "Who's Jim Merriman?"

"*Harrison*," I said. "He's a poet and novelist."

"Oh."

The first day, Saturday, was the two-fly fishing contest. The night before I had gone to a Marcia Ball concert in Boulder. It was too loud (I seem to remember the blues being quieter), I stayed out too late and drank just enough gin and tonics to give me a mild hangover. The rules had specified "normal fishing conditions," right?

I chose a #14 Royal Wulff and a #14 Adams for my flies. Looking back on it, that was an odd choice. I knew the stream pretty well, and knew also that a better choice would have been a brace of #16 St. Vrain Caddis flies, or maybe a caddis for the morning and a small hopper for the afternoon. I think I picked the Adams and the Wulff because of the stance I'd decided to take on this. I was going to compete as a favor to Mike, but I wasn't going to take it seriously and I might just decide to look down on anyone who did.

When we presented our flies to the judges for inspection, everyone else's two flies looked better than mine. There were flawless Hares Ear nymphs (always a good choice), trim Blue-winged Olives (a hatch that could come off at that time of year) and one guy had a beautifully matched pair of #10 Coachman Trudes. I had grabbed my two flies out of a box at the last minute that morning. The Adams was new, but the Wulff looked used.

The actual fishing took place on an eighteen-mile stretch of the South Fork of the St. Vrain. A judge accompanied each fisherman to observe and keep score. There were no assigned beats, you picked your own spots and you could move as often as you wanted to. Scoring was simple: One trout was good for one point, size notwithstanding. Suckers didn't count. All fish had to be released immediately and a bad or clumsy release—one that might injure the fish—would cost you points.

You could fish any rod you wanted as long as it didn't exceed nine feet three-quarters of an inch in length—that is, a nine-foot rod allowing for slop—but you had to use the same rod for all the events, casting as well as fishing. I chose an eight-and-a-half-foot, six-weight bamboo that Mike made for me a few years ago fitted with a weight forward 7 line—a heavier rod than I care to fish on a small stream, but lighter than I'd choose to cast for distance. Either it was the right choice or it put me at a disadvantage in all three events.

I took my judge, Clint, to a stretch of pocket water not far from town, figuring my time would be better spent fishing than driving. I tied my Adams to a 2x, eight-pound-test leader so I wouldn't lose it and began casting. I wanted broken pocket water because the trout there tend to be a little less picky than they are in smoother currents. The heavy leader made the fly drift as if it were wired to a welding rod.

It was a bright, cool, early fall day. The cottonwoods and bigtooth maples along the stream were turning yellow and the dogwoods were red. I got in the water at the bottom of a good-looking pool. Clint found a flat rock in the sun, lay down with his hands behind his head and said, "If you get one, give me a yell."

I decided to work the stream quickly, covering the most water in the shortest possible time. That seemed like the best way to catch lots of fish (remember, size didn't count) and I wanted to keep Clint from taking a nap, which he seemed on the verge of doing. I was still a little hungover, and if I couldn't have a nap, then neither could he.

The Adams wasn't exactly the wrong fly—it never is—but it wasn't entirely right, either. That is, I was hooking a trout now and then, but not as many as I wanted to. I could remember better days on that stream, but that probably wasn't fair. A fisherman's memory is notoriously expansive, and we all know that if a guy says you can catch an average of fifty trout a day on some stream, he's talking about the most fish ever caught there in living memory, plus 10 percent.

More to the point, I figured at least some of the other contestants must be doing better. In the normal course of things I have sometimes wondered how other fishermen were doing, but actually worrying about it was a new experience.

I was happier than usual to see five- and six-inch trout because they were still worth one point, just like a big one, and they were quicker to land. But when I was hand-landing one and it wiggled off the hook (and I didn't get my point because I hadn't actually touched the fish) I started using the landing net. I used it on fish small enough to swim through the mesh.

Just before the scheduled lunch break, I found a little brown trout rising under some overhanging brush on the far bank. It was the kind of situation I'd been passing up, not wanting to snag my only fly, but that close to the break I figured what the hell, I can afford to lose the fly now because I'll get another one after lunch, and if I do this right I'll make another point.

After a few tries I got a nice cast over the fish and he made a classic refusal rise: came up, looked at the fly and turned away. He wanted the St. Vrain caddis pattern I should have picked instead of the stupid Adams. Clint was looking at his watch. The morning session would be over in five minutes.

I thought, Come on you little shit, time is money.

The casting events on Sunday were straightforward. For the distance competition we stood at a chalked line down in Meadow Park and cast as far as we could along a surveyor's tape lying on the grass. We got three casts and all the distances were added together for our score.

We helped each other stretch out our lines and then took some practice casts. There were about twenty people standing around watching. Half of them were asking the other half, "What's going on here?"

The accuracy course consisted of six stations set up in the pretty little stretch of trout stream that runs through the park. At each station the caster stood within three feet of a stake in the water and cast at a number of floating ring targets.

The scoring here was a little complex. You started with one hundred points and then gained points for hits and lost them for misses and ticks. (A "tick" is when your fly hits the water or a branch while you're false casting.) You could also decline a target and lose fewer points than if you tried it and missed a few times.

This was a difficult course set out by cruel judges who didn't have to compete themselves, although I have to say it was realistic. Most of the targets were in places where you might catch a trout in a small stream like this, and there were plenty of overhanging branches and snags to grab your hook-less tournament fly, just like in the real world. Other accuracy courses are sometimes laid out on lawns or open casting pools. This one was a lot more interesting.

And, naturally, there was pressure. A judge stood near each ring, one or two were behind you to watch your back cast and one was on the bank with a clipboard, keeping score. With each cast voices would come from different directions saying "Tick" or "Miss" or occasionally "Hit," while comments drifted over from the small crowd of spectators: things like, "He's not as good as that guy in the blue hat, is he?"

A tournament that accurately represented all the subtleties of fly-fishing doesn't exist and probably never will. It would have to have not only casting and fish-catching competitions, but also categories for fashion (Old World, punk, neon, blue-collar), not to mention lunch and wine selection, the invention and naming of fly patterns, bird and edible plant identification, good-heartedness, humor, lying, trespassing, philosophical detachment, creative misdirection of fellow anglers and so on.

Scoring on anything as obvious as number of fish or total

inches would be ridiculously simple-minded. A big, dumb fish would have to be worth fewer points than a little, smart one, and trout not caught would have to be worth something, too. If you got a large brown in a difficult spot to inspect and refuse five different fly patterns without putting him down, you'd get, say, ten points. If you called him a bastard, your score would remain the same, but if you *meant* it, you'd lose five points.

If the event was scheduled for a day that happened to be bright and sunny, you'd have to get at least one hundred points for declaring that you were going to stay home, patch the canoe and wait for a cloudy day to fish.

It would also have to be possible for a guy who caught no fish to beat a guy who caught twenty. He could do it by getting skunked with good humor while fishing a hundred-year-old bamboo rod, wearing creatively patched waders and having elk paté on melba toast and Thunderbird wine for lunch. Or maybe he could make up enough points in the Zen category by honestly not caring or, better yet, fishing without a fly as an exercise in meditation and then saying to the judges afterward, "Well, catching trout and not catching trout really amount to the same thing, right?"

All fish would have to be released immediately, unless you had a really neat recipe and found some wild mushrooms along the stream to go with it. Extra points would be awarded if you cooked the fish on site, but if the mushrooms turned out to be poisonous, you'd be disqualified.

If you won the tournament and the check for your entry fee bounced a day later, you would also receive the special Board of Governors' No Visible Means of Support Award. A small trophy would also go to the judge who was the least judgmental.

For a long time now I've said I didn't like fly-fishing contests because they seem unnatural, and now that I've fished in one, I can say that with even more conviction. That is, *I* don't like them. You, of course, can make up your own mind.

For the record, I came in dead third in all three events in a very small field of competitors. Afterward Mike said, "Well, I guess that makes you the third best fly fisherman in Colorado," which he and I both know is pretty damned far from the truth.

On a personal level, I came very close to wishing ill on a friend. At lunch on Saturday, I learned that Dale Darling was several fish (points, that is) ahead of me. Dale is a good fisherman and he knows that stream as well as anyone, so it was unlikely that he'd use the wrong fly in the afternoon session or be unable to locate trout. I didn't exactly hope he'd slip on a wet rock and break his casting arm, but I allowed as how that would be to my advantage.

So what does that mean? If there was a quarter-million-dollar purse at stake, would I have had a crew of hired henchmen out there greasing all the rocks?

The prize here was the custom bamboo fly rod of your choice from Mike Clark and a little bit of glory—both worth having, although the former is probably worth more and will certainly last longer than the latter. Having decided not to take this contest seriously, I guess I failed when it occurred to me that it would actually be kind of neat to win.

Okay, so there's a kind of openheartedness about these things that I never learned. That's why I fish instead of playing on a local softball team. Sports that require two teams or two players for a match or where the participants gamble with their own money are *about* competition, but fly-fishing is solitary, contemplative, misanthropic, scientific in some hands, poetic in others and laced with conflicting aesthetic considerations. It's not even clear if catching fish is actually the point. I just don't think you can shoehorn all that into the great American misconception that life consists of a few champions and a whole bunch of losers.

And then there's the cuteness factor. In a sense, the one

or two fly business is as necessary as the sack in a sack race, but in fact one of the keys to catching trout is the ability to assess the situation and change from the fly that was right five minutes ago to the fly that's right now, not to mention the knowledge and forethought it takes to have those flies with you.

If competition dishonors the game, what does engineered silliness do to the competitors? On the other hand, if you're worried about your dignity, are you taking yourself too seriously? Does competition trivialize fly-fishing? Is it possible to trivialize something that, at its best, shouldn't be that important? I'd say a *real* fly fisherman would never stoop so low as to compete with his colleagues, except that that would be the most sanctimonious statement I've ever made.

Not long ago a man called and asked me to enter a contest they were having over on the West Slope. They were going to field a bunch of two-person teams composed of a fly fisherman and a golfer. One day you fished, the next day you played eighteen holes. It was all for an unspecified good cause and there was supposed to be lots of press coverage.

"I don't golf," I said.

"No, see, that's the point," the guy said. "You don't golf, and you'll be paired with a golfer who doesn't fish, so you'll both have the opportunity to make fools of yourselves. They're gonna videotape it. It'll be a hoot!"

"You don't understand," I said, "I am philosophically *opposed* to golf."

16

West

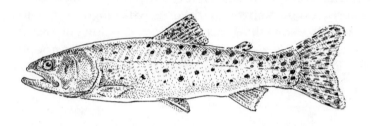

Not long ago A.K. Best and I found ourselves in West Yellowstone, Montana, on what we'll call, for official purposes, a business trip.

The Federation of Fly Fishers Conclave was in town, and Jim Criner, now owner of Bud Lilly's Trout Shop, asked us to come up and sign copies of our books in the store for a couple of mornings. Mornings, that is, so we could sneak out and fish in the afternoons. He also said he'd put us up and we could stay as long as we liked. Jim had thought this through. He understood we weren't going to be on expense accounts from our publishers, so he felt we might need a little incentive to make the thirteen-hour drive from Colorado.

The book signings were actually very successful, but there were still some of those inevitable doldrums to get through. A good way to stay humble about being a writer is to sit at a table with your life's work in front of you and wait for, say, an hour and a half for an adoring fan to show up. Finally a guy does walk over. He smiles and says, "Hi, you got a public toilet here?"

Some years ago A.K. and I both spent time working in fly shops, so when there didn't happen to be anyone wanting an autograph, our tendency was to go on automatic: helping people try on waders and select flies, which beats sitting around trying to be famous when things are slow.

I also bought a new hat from the shop. A few weeks before, while we were camped at Roy Palm's place on the Frying Pan River in Colorado, Roy's sweet little bird dog pup had eaten my old one.

I wouldn't have kicked the dog even if she wasn't worth a reported four thousand dollars and even if Roy hadn't been very good to me over the years. Puppies will be puppies and fishing hats, even old favorite ones, are expendable. The only thing that bothered me was, a new fishing hat cost almost forty dollars. I must be getting old. I remember when you could buy a Hardy reel for forty dollars.

In fact, that's about what a good fly reel went for the first time I came to West Yellowstone in the 1970s, back when Bud Lilly still owned Bud Lilly's Trout Shop. There's a gentrified covered mall in town now (at least it's small) and at a neat little bookstore called the Book Peddler you can actually get a cup of cappuccino, but aside from a few things like that, the place hasn't changed much. It's still a small, funky, honestly rustic, somewhat touristy, largely one-story western town that grew up haphazardly at the west entrance to Yellowstone National Park.

When mail first started arriving there in 1908, the town— or at least the post office—was called Riverside. The following year it was changed to Yellowstone and then, in 1920, it became *West* Yellowstone. Now, in regional anglers' shorthand, it's often referred to simply as "West."

West Yellowstone is arguably the capital city of American fly-fishing. It's a town with 924 year-round residents that supports five fly shops, countless guides and fly tiers and the

Federation of Fly Fishers international headquarters. Not every business in town has stuffed trout on the walls, but those that don't seem oddly stark. World famous western trout rivers like the Madison, Yellowstone, Gibbon, Firehole and Henry's Fork, not to mention many lesser-known streams and lakes, are within easy day-trip range.

The trout-fishing in the area is wonderful, or, fishing being what it is, let's say it *can* be when the conditions are right. Whether it's as fabulous as it once was is a matter of some debate. There's always the suspicion that it was better in the good old days and Al McClane, one of the early jet set angling writers and an undisputed expert in such matters, has said, "Montana fishing has survived as well as can be expected against the onslaught of civilization."

Then again, Bud Lilly, who was born in that country and should know, said, "When the fishing around West Yellowstone started to get a lot of attention from the fishing writers in the late 1960s and early 1970s, those of us who lived there noticed a surprising increase in the size of fish being reported (but not seen or photographed) from some rivers."

It's a scandalous implication, but then fishermen—let alone writers—*have* been known to exaggerate.

So let's just say that the fishing is better than average at the very least and, more important, it is legendary. Even if the trout you catch are only a few inches longer than the ones you get back home, they are nonetheless from rivers that are, as they say, part of the literature of the sport. That's important. In certain circles, the names of famous rivers can be dropped as impressively as those of movie stars.

So fly-fishing in the West Yellowstone area amounts to a kind of pilgrimage. An unofficial survey of license plates reveals that most of the visitors are from states west of the Mississippi, but you see plates from all over—Florida, Kentucky, Maine, pick a place—and in years past I've run into anglers from England, Australia, Germany, Japan and New Zealand.

One of the New Zealanders, with a deadpan delivery worthy of a native Montanan, said he was having a nice time, even though, compared to back home, the beer was watery and the trout were small.

When I asked Vicki Eggers at the West Yellowstone Chamber of Commerce how many fishermen the town saw in a season, she said she couldn't say, but it was "a sizable number." To the same question, a fly shop owner or a guide will say, "Plenty," and a fisherman may say, "Too many."

Even if you didn't know beforehand, you'd spot this as a fishing town before you'd driven two blocks. Maybe it's the businesses that cater to anglers in one way or another or all the obvious fishing vehicles, ranging from official-looking pickups towing Mackenzie boats to decrepit Volkswagens with float tubes strapped on top.

Or maybe it's the fishermen themselves. As you walk or drive down the main drag, you keep thinking you see people you know, but before you can turn to whomever you're with and say, "Isn't that. . . ?" you realize it's not the specific person you recognize, but the type: ageless—say, forty on up—male or female, fit, tanned, dressed in a practical, sporting sort of way, often wearing the expression Ed Engle calls the hundred-mile stare. Fly fishers. It's hard to explain, but they don't have to be wearing hip boots. You pick them out the way members of any subculture can spot each other pretty much at a glance.

And it works the other way around, too. I can't remember ever buying gas, coffee or anything else in West without being asked, "How's the fishing?" I don't know how they can tell I'm not there to look at the geysers; it's just obvious somehow.

Of course, sometimes you do recognize someone, either a friend from somewhere or one of the many angling celebrities who show up in town on a fairly regular basis. On any street corner or in any bar, café or fly shop you might spot Ernest Schweibert, Doug Swisher, Gary LaFontaine, Nick Lyons, Dave Whitlock or almost any other face you've seen on the dust jacket of a fly-fishing book. In years past it might have been Lee Wulff or Arnold Gingrich. Everyone shows up there sooner or later.

I've been told that angling notoriety is the best kind in that, although certain people may know who you are, you can still walk down any street in any town in the country without being recognized—except maybe in West.

A.K. and I did slip out those first two afternoons. We drove the ninety-mile round trip to a place we know on the Yellowstone River in the park and dragged back into West between 10:30 and 11:00 at night, just in time to get supper at Thiem's Café.

When we arrived in town we'd asked a couple of local contacts the two questions one must have answered immediately, namely, where are the fish biting and what is the current fisherman's café? Both things change from time to time. The consensus was, the Madison and Yellowstone rivers, and Thiem's.

The right café must be casual and cozy (pine paneling is nice, but optional), have good food served in generous portions, have quick service (at least in the morning when you're in a hurry), have waiters and waitresses who can stand up to the endless, corny wisecracks, and keep fishermen's hours.

It also helps if the place has the proper history. Thiem's, like many other establishments in West, displays the obligatory collection of snapshots dating back at least to the 1950s showing the building in winter. On the wall near the bathroom door there are shots of Thiem's—formerly Chat's, formerly Huck's—buried in snow up to the eaves, with just the sign visible at the top of the drift. If no one gets married or catches a huge trout, this might be the only photograph a West Yellowstonian takes in a year. It's a way locals have of reminding us summer tourists that we're dilettantes compared to those who spend their winters there.

The right café provides not only food, but gossip. It's rare for a fisherman you don't know well to tell you precisely where he caught a lot of big trout and what fly he was using, but it's just as rare for him to be able to entirely contain himself if he's done well. Consequently, if you pay attention and read between the lines, you can deduce that certain insect hatches are on and that people are generally "doing okay" on a stretch of a certain river roughly between this bridge and that roadhouse. This is B-list stuff, but valuable just the same.

You can also learn who's staying in whose spare cabin, guest room or back porch, borrowing whose drift boat or guiding for which shop, although trying to look anyone up is usually a waste of time. Someone you know may be "in town," but of course that's a euphemism. They're actually out fishing, dawn till dusk, and if they're into something good, they probably didn't tell anyone where they were going. You learn to say, "Well, maybe we'll run into him."

And you really do want to run into him because it's the people you know who give you the best tips about where there are big fish that are currently biting and that everyone isn't onto: the *A*-list material. There can be mobs of fishermen in and around West in the summer, but there are also countless miles of good water in the immediate area, which, depending on how hard you want to drive, includes the park (which is in Wyoming), a good chunk of Montana and a sizable corner of Idaho. There are always secrets to be learned.

Around West, the best fishing tips often come with the standard boilerplate grizzly disclaimer: "You park at the bridge, cross the river, hike downstream until the trail peters out, then go on for another two miles and start fishing at the big bend in the river. Now, there *are* some bears down there . . ."

This is done for a number of reasons. First, there really are a few grizzlies around, although they're hardly ever seen. Statistically, your chances of getting stomped by a bison or hit by a car are far greater than those of being attacked by a bear, but it does happen, and a bear attack can be extremely definitive. If you sent some tenderfoot to a fishing spot where grizzlies had been seen a time or two over the last few seasons and a week later the search party turned up a broken fly rod and a single, bloody hiking boot, you might feel a little funny about it if you hadn't issued the usual warning. So local etiquette demands that you say, "Now, there *are* some bears down there . . ." so if anything happens it won't be your fault.

And I think there's also a subtle character check involved. When a guy gives up a great spot, he wants to think you're worthy of it. If a little thing like a grizzly bear is going to scare you off, it's probably just as well.

In some hands this whole bear business can be yet another one of those subtle digs that locals really do have a right to. Sure, you had a good trip and caught lots of trout, but a competent local smart-ass can send you home thinking you probably could have gotten into even bigger fish if you'd only had more guts.

I guess you just have to understand the relationship between the residents of a tourist town and the tourists themselves. Locals can be like cowboys: They may love the life and the region, but they can eventually get tired of the cows.

People who like trout have the same kind of affection for West that other people have for, say, Paris. That is, it begins as a kind of cultural conditioning before we've even seen the place, and then once we've been there a few times we begin to feel like honorary citizens, strolling its sidewalks with a proprietary air. After all, we're fly fishermen, and this is a fly-fishing town.

To be honest, we tend to look down a little on the regular tourists who only come to view the wildlife from the car and maybe do some shopping in town because they are there as spectators, while we're there to participate. Granted, fly fishers are an arrogant bunch as a rule, but when people stop their cars, run down to take your picture while you're fishing, and then ask you things like, "Where do they keep the buffalo in the winter?" it's hard not to feel a little superior.

On the other hand, I can't say I know the town itself well. Over the past fifteen years or so, I've been in all the fly shops, some of the gas stations and cafés, the Laundromat, a book store and the post office. Once, years ago, a bunch of us rented a room in the Alpine Motel for an afternoon so we could take showers, but we didn't stay the night, and I have now had a cup of authentic West Yellowstone cappuccino, which was real good.

I'm told there are one or two decent restaurants, but I've never eaten in them because they don't stay open late enough. On this last trip, one of our publishers told A.K. and me that, although he wouldn't spring for the trip, he would reimburse us for a dinner. We wanted to stick him good—and he fully expected that—but the best we could do was a couple of chicken fried steak specials at Thiem's.

I can't remember offhand the numbers of the highways leading out of town in three directions, but I know where they go. To the east is the road into the park that takes you to the Firehole, upper Madison, Yellowstone and such. The road north goes to Bozeman and the Gallatin River, crossing the Madison, Cougar Creek, Duck Creek and so on. (Duck Creek is pretty good, but there *are* some bears.) The Idaho Road goes south, toward the Henry's Fork and beyond.

Like most fishermen who show up in West on a more or less regular basis to eat, sleep, buy trout flies and ask directions, I know the surrounding rivers better than the town. That's not to say I'm anything but a normal duffer, but I've been there often enough—and been out with enough good guides—that I do have some spots.

A "spot" doesn't have to be remote (some good ones are within sight of roads) and it doesn't have to be completely unknown. It just has to be a good place to fish that isn't a

regular stop for half the guides and fly fishers in three states;
a place you stand a fair chance of having all to yourself and
that you wouldn't tell just anyone about.

Like that stretch of the Yellowstone A.K. and I know about.
It's miles from the famous spots on that river that everyone
fishes. There are fewer cutthroat trout there, but they are bigger and healthier. A friend who spends his summers in West
took us there years ago, but we now think of it as our spot.
In all the time we've been fishing it we've seen two other anglers and a bull moose.

That's not to say we always catch fish there. Once a guide
asked me if catching those big, dumb cutthroats in the Yellowstone wasn't a little like shooting fish in a barrel. I had
to say, "Not to me."

We fished that spot those first two afternoons after the
book signings and we caught some nice big trout. Then on
the second night, over buffalo burgers at Thiem's, we ran
into an East Coast guide that A.K. knows. A.K. is a professional fly tier and by now he knows half the people in the
business.

This guy knew we'd been fishing the area off and on for
quite a few years, so he naturally assumed we knew what
we were doing. After all, fly-fishing is one small part of American culture where it's still assumed that experience and a
little age naturally bring wisdom. After the usual pleasantries,
the guy asked how we'd been doing—the standard opening
move.

"Oh," I said, "we've been getting into some fish," trying to
sound as if, you know, we'd been holding up our end, but it
was nothing really fabulous or anything, while at the same
time leaving open the possibility that it *had* been fabulous
and I was just being cagey.

"Where?" the guy asked casually, and A.K. answered, "On
the Yellowstone," glancing at me now because we were getting into a sensitive area.

"Oh," the guide said, "where exactly on the Yellowstone?"
At this point in these classic, ticklish conversations, the

questioner usually gives up on innocence (he knows he's just asked an impertinent question) and tries for just the right note of brazenness. The interviewee is then faced with either telling him or ending it right there without being too rude.

A.K. looked up from his buffalo burger and said, with finality, "Not where you think."

By now we have a handful of places like this between us. Most were gifts from friends, a precious few are ours alone and were hard won. We don't tell other visitors about them because we don't want the word to get around, and we don't tell locals for fear these spots aren't as secret as we think they are. In this town you want to feel plugged into the local fly-fishing mystique, if only for a week or so out of every summer, and nothing will deflate you quicker than hearing someone say, "Oh, hell, everyone knows about *that*."

So we assume that recognizable West Yellowstone pose: modest, seasoned and ever so slightly self-satisfied. The implication being, yes, I guess we do know a thing or two about the fishing around here, and, no, we don't really care to go into it. If nothing else, we know how to fit in here. We understand that the less you say about fly-fishing, the more people will assume you know.

17

Night

I'm like most fishermen when it comes to night fishing: I know something about it (or at least I'm familiar with the mythology) but I don't actually go out and do it much, if only because it takes a sharpness that's hard for me to muster up at the end of the day.

I'm essentially diurnal, like most modern humans, and too often I feel as if night is a different, unfamiliar place where I don't feel at home. But then that's a thought I have coming off the river at dusk or maybe in camp in the evening, enclosed in my little dome of firelight; the idea that by dark you should *be* somewhere. Once you get out in it, night isn't really that foreign. It's more like a large room in your own house where, for reasons of habit, you seldom go.

I'm talking about real night now, not illuminated city or suburban, controlled-environment, flick-of-a-switch night. You know, the kind where it actually gets dark and things are different.

One of the best reasons I can think of for being active at night is that many of the fish we like to chase in the daytime are at least partly nocturnal, and some of them, like large-mouth bass and brown trout, are notorious for it. In some places, the really big fish can take to feeding exclusively under cover of darkness and they'll be seen in daylight only when spawning or, rarely, when there's some fabulous feeding opportunity like a salmon fly or Green Drake hatch.

When you see these big fish where you never saw them before, your first thought is, Where did they come from? But deep down you know they're just shy; you know they're really always there to be caught every night. It's *you* who've been missing.

Like most common wisdom, this is correct often enough, but an honest night fisher will be the first to tell you it doesn't always work. The fish don't always bite, and when they do it's not always the big ones. Good fishing depends on so many things: water temperature, stream flow, turbidity, insect lifecycles, time of year, the phase of the moon (both for the light it sheds and, perhaps, for more mysterious reasons). In actual fact, night fishing is a lot like day fishing, except you can't see what you're doing.

I'm always tantalized by the idea of big fish, but what I really enjoy about night fishing is being out with the owls, bats, rabbits, deer, raccoons and such. Half the natural world is nocturnal, and sometimes I get to thinking about how much I miss by sleeping when it's dark. And there's also a pleasant surreptitious feeling to it—"under cover of darkness" and all that. It's almost like poaching but without the moral dilemma or the possibility of getting caught.

I'm a typical, more or less civilized, late-twentieth-century light junkie, so I'm naturally a little apprehensive about being out at night, but I know it's not the actual darkness that's dangerous, only the possible results of it. I could bump into something, fall down, walk off a high bank, wade into barbed wire or get lost. This is a subtle but important distinction: I know the darkness itself is not going to swallow me up.

The last time I went night fishing was in August on the Roaring Fork River in Colorado. A few of us had been fishing the Green Drake and Pale Morning Dun mayfly hatches on the nearby Frying Pan: pretty, daytime, highly visual stuff. After a few good days of this, Roy Palm—whose land we were camping on—said he and one of his guides were going to go night fish a spot they have on the Fork and asked if we wanted to come along.

I, for one, almost always accept invitations like that. Roy has lived for many years now within sight of one great trout river and very near another. He's a guide and he owns the Frying Pan Angler fly shop in Basalt. At least half of the hot local fly patterns for the area originally came from Roy's vise. He may not know everything about the fishing thereabouts, but I doubt anyone knows more.

And it's also just a general principle that when the boys at the fly shop ask you to join them after hours at an unspecified place they know of, the only proper response is, "Okay, where and when?" Good guides will always go the full distance to put their clients into the best fishing, with just one footnote: If only to keep themselves interested, they'll hold a little something back for themselves. Night fishing is custom made for that because it's something most sports wouldn't want to do anyway.

We slogged down to the river through an overgrown stretch of swampy wetland that was hard going even with a little light left in the sky. The faint trail we were on wound around several odd-shaped ponds, and I could see that on the way back I'd come on a couple of forks that went off in different directions. I tried to think, okay, left, right, and then left again, reversed, of course, because I'll be going the other way coming out, but I knew I'd forget that too soon. There'd be the beam of a pocket flashlight to help, but that doesn't do as much for you as you'd think. That small, lit-up piece of trail could be anywhere. It's like having someone quote a random passage from a book you read once and trying to guess what page it's on. I decided to locate one of the people I was with when it was time to leave. Two of these guys were locals who would, presumably, know the way out.

That particular stretch of river was wide and fast, with the kind of slick, cobbled bottom fishermen like to call "greased cannon balls"—tricky to wade even when you can see what you're doing. But the stream bed dropped off quickly where I was, so I figured at least some fish would be working close to shore and I wouldn't have to wade too far out.

In fact, isn't that what's supposed to happen at night? Aren't the big fish supposed to move out of the mysterious depths and into the shallows just a roll cast away? That's the theory, but I've seen fishing theories come up short. I remember thinking I should either do more of this or not mess with it at all.

There were about twenty yards of slower current between the bank and the river's main channel that I figured to be the fishable water. I tried to get a picture of that in my mind, as well as one of the thick stand of willows behind me. I'd have to remember to keep my back cast high.

These are the logistical matters you think about at dusk, when you can still see.

The word was there might be a good night caddis hatch here, but that had been carefully offered without a guarantee. Caddis hatches can be spooky and guides like to hedge their bets, even when they're off duty.

There were a few small caddis flies swarming over the water in the last light—not a proper hatch, but a good sign—so I began with a #14 Elk Hair Caddis dry fly. That was a size or two larger than the naturals, but this is acceptable. There's something about night fishing that changes the scale of things and lets you fish larger flies. In fact, there's one school of thought that says if the trout are feeding on a #16 caddis, you should tie on a #2 Muddler Minnow.

This was a pretty spot. The Roaring Fork is a big, wide river for Colorado, and it seems to get bigger, not to mention louder, at night. Behind me was the swamp and the thick little grove of willows. To the west, where the river turned sharply, was a high cliff above a bend pool that looked bottomless. To the east was a line of rocky hills that I knew to be bright red with scattered green juniper and pine, but by then the colors were quickly bleeding out of things and it was all becoming shades of gray.

Across the river—maybe seventy-five yards wide there—were the sloping, rocky pastures, barbed-wire fences and crooked, unpainted outbuildings of a sheep ranch. I could hear sheep bleating peacefully—a sound that's been called the coyote's dinner bell—and I thought I could just make some of them out over there, although the gray bumps I saw could have been rocks.

When one of the bumps began to move I thought, Sheep. Then, when I saw the ambling way it walked, I revised that to sheep*dog*.

I began casting upstream, working the water in a fan pattern starting parallel to the bank and working out into the main current. Operating on some vision of thoroughness, I'd do this twice before taking a few steps and doing the same thing again. Thinking of that grayish-olive wall of willows, I was trying to approximate a steeple cast, keeping the line high behind me. I thought I could hear trout rising, but I couldn't be sure. A big river makes a lot of noise: a large overall rush with scattered plops and gurgles. When you're fishing a dry fly on a dead drift, you set the hook on any plop that sounds unusually definitive. Sometimes there's a fish there, but usually all you feel is the loose tug and slide of your line against the water.

After an indeterminate amount of time (time changes in

the dark, too) I reeled in and, with the help of a small flash-light, clipped off the little caddis pattern and tied on the biggest dry fly I could find, a #8 or #10 Royal Trude with an inch-long white calf tail wing. I turned my back to the river to keep the flashlight beam off the water. I don't know if this is really necessary or not, but several night fishers have told me it is. If nothing else, it probably doesn't hurt.

The logic for big flies at night has always seemed shaky to me. Are there larger bugs on the water at night than there are in the daytime? Not usually, and when there are, this is typically well-known among the local anglers. Still, it works, the theory being that fish can see a big fly well at night and, under the cover of darkness, they become greedy and reckless.

Ideally, a night fly should be black because after dark color means little or nothing. The trout are looking upward through whorly currents into faint starlight, so what you want is the darkest, sharpest silhouette possible: black. And when you think of it that way, sure, big too.

Another theory calls for a black body with a big white wing for visibility, but that can't be right. Your eyes become accustomed to the darkness, and starlight does faintly outline the top halves of certain objects with a dull, colorless glow, but I defy anyone to say he can actually see the white wing of a fly thirty yards out on a mostly black river filled with the shifting dull silver bumps of the current.

I have tied night flies—big, bushy, all-black hair-wing jobs, often with a thin silver tinsel rib on the body because I think that looks elegant—but I never make very many and they're the last ones I replace when the fly boxes are getting low, so I'm often caught without them. I tied on the big Trude because it was the closest thing I had to what I wanted. Then I turned off the little flashlight and stood for a few minutes to let my eyes get accustomed to the darkness again. I felt the wings of a bug tickle my cheek just above the beard and tried to picture the air filled with caddis flies and the water boiling with trout.

I listened for it, but all I could make out was water moving. I did once hear a caddis hatch at night. The flies were large, the night was still and the river was slow and quiet. There was a soft hum with liquid blips in it and the slicing of bats' wings. It was very much like the sound I once heard, years ago, after being hit very hard in the face by a guy with whom I had a small misunderstanding.

A few minutes later I hooked and landed one modest-sized trout. I think it was a brown and I think it was about a foot long, although I can't be sure on either count because I hand-landed it and released it by feel. You don't want to use the flashlight unless you have to because every time you turn it off again you are lost and blinded for a while.

I couldn't remember why I'd set the hook on that fish. It wasn't dumb luck, though, because I could recall hearing that internal command: "Set now." I could fish for another fifty years and never get used to the surprise of guessing right.

I thought surely the caddis hatch was going good. Now and then other flies brushed my face or the backs of my hands or bopped my canvas hat, and when you extrapolate that to thousands of cubic feet of cool, summer air over one of the best trout rivers in the state, you have to imagine the hatch of a lifetime. But you do have to imagine it.

Sometime later I made a short cast upstream and heard a splash more or less in that direction. It was not a sound the current had made in the last couple of hours. I raised the rod tip and, sure enough, there was the weight of a fish. At a time like that you naturally wonder how many strikes you didn't hear.

This seemed like a heavy trout, but it was hard to tell for sure because he immediately bored out into the fast water and took off downstream, peeling line from the reel. I may have shouted something because the sheepdog across the river started to bark.

I was using an eight-and-a-half-foot, six-weight rod with

a weight forward 7 line, something stout for the possible large trout, and the kind of rod you can get away with at night when delicacy isn't an issue. This is an old favorite rod and I thought I could judge the weight of the trout by the heft of it, but in fast current like that you usually feel more water than fish.

Moments like this have a familiar resonance that seems to go beyond what's happening right then, and I wish I could hand the rod to one of those people who ask, "What *is* it that gets you guys so cranked up about fishing, anyway?"

The fish is out there somewhere, one of many, but this one is now potentially yours. It has a mind of its own, but, although you haven't captured it yet, you have a tentative grip on it. You know what it is, but there's still a lot you don't know. It's *probably* a trout, although it could be a whitefish, in which case there will be some disappointment. At this point you can only guess at its size and weight.

Here is a thing you want—at the moment, it's a fish, but this exact same feeling could be about love, success, long life or whatever. You have hold of it with a good rod and a big enough hook, but you can't see what you're doing and you know it's not going to come to you like a puppy.

I let the fish run downstream and carefully eased him out of the current into the quieter water near the bank. When the weight of the river went off the line, there still seemed to be a lot left. Then, trying to keep the line tight, I stumbled and felt my way down to him.

When I got close he shot out into the current again and made another wide loop downstream. I tried to stay out of the water to make better time, but feeling along in the dark puts you at about the same pace as wading, so it didn't make much difference. My right foot would splash shallow water, and then five steps farther on my left shoulder would be brushed by willow leaves, so I knew I was weaving.

I thought I was getting close to the big pool at the bottom

of that cliff, and I knew that if the fish ran downstream from there I wouldn't be able to follow and probably couldn't winch him back up through the current. I tried to feel the shape of the bank curving out, but I didn't know exactly where the bank was. There was a riffle at the head of that bend pool that I thought I should hear when I got close. I *didn't* hear it, so maybe it was still okay. Then again, I didn't know how far out the fish was.

I felt my reel to try to see how much line was left on it, but it was hard to picture. Some, maybe lots.

The fish let himself be played back against the bank again. I couldn't hear the riffle and I hadn't felt the rush of it in the line, so I knew he was in slack water where I could get at him. I waded down—I was in the water, although I didn't remember getting in—and fumbled for the net when the angle of the line seemed to indicate the fish was more or less at my feet.

I made a mess of netting him, thinking I knew where he was, only to come up two or three times with a dripping but empty landing net. I finally managed it with the rod in my left hand, net in my right and the flashlight in my teeth.

It was a brown trout, not a bright, golden yellow one, but a washed-out, older fish; brownish ochre on the back shading to an almost bluish silver with big black spots. He'd fought like a five-pounder, but in the net he looked and felt more like four. And, yes, weight and length change at night, too. Maybe he was more like twenty inches and a fat three pounds, but he was my fish and it hurt a little to let him go.

I was stumbling back upstream, thinking I could keep fishing the dry fly, switch to the biggest black Woolly Bugger streamer I had or quit while I was ahead. A nice big fish can seem like a proper end to things, especially when it's well past midnight and you've been fishing since seven o'clock on what would now be *yesterday* morning.

Then I ran into one of my hosts, who was wading downstream looking for me. He was a big shape with a hat and I couldn't tell who it was until he spoke. He asked how I'd done.

"I got a nice one," I said, and he didn't ask how nice, knowing that this isn't always easy to explain. Instead he said, "Do you remember where the trail back to the car is?"

18

One Fish

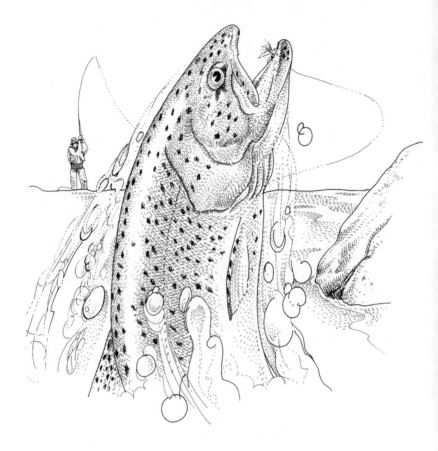

I want to tell you about one fish I caught recently. I'll be bragging here, but I feel I deserve that. It's so seldom I get everything right.

This happened on a river in Colorado during a great Pale Morning Dun mayfly hatch. There's a stretch of braided

pocket water a few miles downstream from a catch and release area that's known to guides and locals as Old Faithful,
not so much because the fishing is easy, but because the
hatches are good there and trout rise dependably.

I was on the river with Steve Binder and Ed Engle, and the
first day we fished the Old Faithful stretch I spent an hour
or so in a spot I knew to be especially difficult. I guess I
could say I took the hard spot and left the easier stretches
for my two friends, but that would be misleading.

The thing is, there's a secret hidden in difficult water. It's
hard to fish, but because of that a lot of people pass it up
and a lot of other people fish it poorly and catch nothing.
Consequently, if you can get a good cast in there and a reasonable drift, the fish are actually—in a convoluted sort of
way—pretty easy to hook. And there's also a fair chance
they'll be big, strong, healthy and unscarred.

This spot has a wide, dangerously fast, thigh-deep rip on
the near side, a long, narrow tongue of slower current beyond that where the flow is broken by a big, red rock, then
another rip and then a complicated plunge pool where three
separate currents spill in, one fast and deep, the others
smaller and slower.

I'd learned in past years that if you could wade out far
enough in the rip, you could throw a slack cast with an upstream mend into that first narrow glide and get a good dry
fly drift. I'd also learned that this was worth doing because
lots of trout would stack up in there during a hatch.

So I did that, caught four or five trout and missed or
spooked twice that many more. Then I got to looking at the
plunge pool on the far side of the river that, for some reason, I'd never paid much attention to before. There were
some mayflies floating on the surface over there and every
now and then—if you stood and watched long enough—a
large head would show in one place or another as what
looked like a pod of several large trout ate the flies.

It was the kind of spot that looked impossible, calling for
a long cast that would have to loop the line upstream and

then down in half a dozen places and then pile two feet of leader to allow a dry fly to dead-drift six inches or so. You've seen places like that on trout streams before. The currents are so complex and confused that the water sometimes seems to stand still and tremble, not knowing where to go next, but in fact it's moving very fast.

I could see that if I got over to the far side of the rip it would be a little easier, but I'd already waded out as far as I could get without being washed downstream, and even where I was, the footing was a little unsure.

I made the cast anyway, out of curiosity. It was the best snake-curve, multiple up-and-downstream hook, pile cast I could muster, but the fly ripped through the pool, leaving a wide wake and apparently spooking the fish. I stood there watching for a long time but, although the flies kept coming, there were no more rises.

The next day we got in the river a little farther upstream and, when the hatch began to come off, I headed down to my spot. The night before in camp—somewhere in the middle of a loud discussion about money, politics and the media—I'd told Ed and Steve about the fish and said I was going to get over there for a better cast even at the risk of drowning. (By the next morning, having developed a more rested, calculating kind of excitement about it, I thought maybe I'd find an easier place to cross.)

This, by the way, is the main difference between the guys you're with and strangers: You don't describe a place like this to someone you meet in a bar for fear that the next day you'll find him standing in your spot, but your friends will leave it for you—at least this one time.

While I was looking for a place to wade across and not locating an easy one, I found an old broom handle on the bank that someone had been using as a wading staff. Whoever had had this thing last had carved a crude notch around one end to hold a cord, and the other end was mashed where it had been pushed against wet rocks. No telling if they'd lost it or just thrown it away. I picked it up and showed it to Ed, who was just wading by at the time. He said matter-of-factly, "That is a gift from the gods."

So with the help of the stick I got over to the other side of the rip. It wasn't really that hard and I might have made it even without a staff. Then again, I might not have. I have this old bad knee that has made me a careful wader. It's kept me from some fish, but it's probably also saved my ass more than once.

When I got where I wanted to be, I saw that I'd been wrong about the pod of big trout. There was actually only one large, fat rainbow, and he was cruising around in what appreared to be random patterns in a pool roughly four or five yards square. The currents were even more conflicting and braided than they'd seemed from the other side of the river, but up close like that I could make shorter casts, keep more line off the water and stand a much better chance.

By this time the mayflies were roaring out of the current in the main channel and at least a dozen trout were rising steadily, but back in the plunge pool there were only a few of them at any one time, so this big trout was cruising widely. He'd take a fly and then noodle around the pool looking for another one. You could tell when he saw a bug because he'd straighten out purposefully and glide over to take it. He seemed to be able to spot them from as far away as two feet.

All I could do was keep my fly in the air by false casting, wait for the fish to rise, see which direction he headed in next and then try to put the fly in front of him. I knew he'd spook if the fly started to drag, so just before the currents grabbed my leader on every cast, I'd have to pick it up, even if the fish was heading right for it.

The trout was wandering all around the pool, and as often as not he'd be in a spot where I didn't think I could get a fair drift. When he worked his way into a relatively easy spot, I'd put the fly down for a few seconds. The rest of the time I just stood there false casting and remembering my uncle Leonard saying, "If you wanna catch fish, you gotta have your hook in the water."

Without going into even more detail, I'll just say that after I don't know how long it all came together, the fish ate the fly and I hooked him. He fought beautifully, jumping once and making a couple of what would have been reel-screaming runs except that I was fishing with a Peerless fly reel that doesn't scream so much as it purrs.

I didn't measure the fish, but I'll guess him at a heavy nineteen or maybe even twenty inches. I took a quick snapshot and released him. He seemed tired, but okay. Then I waded over to a convenient rock and sat down for a while. Catching a big, difficult trout after two days is the kind of thing you have to get straight about.

At first it's a glorious rush of egotism and you begin to feel like death from above. Then you allow that, although you *are* getting to be a pretty damned good fisherman, there was still that element of dumb luck about it. A dozen things could have conspired against getting the right drift at the moment the fish was there to see it, and even then he might have decided he didn't like the fly or he might have taken a natural right next to it. In other words, the spiritually profitable attitude here is not pride but humility.

Of course, wondering how you should feel about this gets you into the area of why you fish in the first place. That's always been an interesting question to me, but I'm beginning to think the only people who really care are a handful of writers and some idly curious nonanglers. The fishermen who don't worry about it are the ones who seem to be having the most fun.

Maybe fishermen are more like cowboys than they appear to be. I've just been reading *The Muddy Fork & Other Things*, in which author James Crumly says that a cowboy is just someone who got up on a horse and never learned how to get down. In this case, it would be a guy who caught a fish one day, thought it was pretty neat, and that was that: no mystique, no real reason.

Or maybe it's some kind of stubborn, unreasoning pride. Fishermen certainly have that, and Crumly says that the cowboys he knows eventually ended up with skin cancer, crippling arthritis, broken bones and no money, but, "They pitied everybody who couldn't live the cowboy life."

It's tempting to launch a psycho-sociological theory here about the fly fisher as cowboy in modern American sporting mythology, but then my old friend A.K. says the proper response to hooking a big, difficult trout is the most primitive one you're capable of, or, as he puts it, "Me fool fish."

So maybe what you should do when you catch a great trout is go back to camp and make a pot of coffee because there will not be a bigger or better fish today. Sooner or later your partners will wander in and you can tell them all about it. That's your reward: a potentially great story that you may be able to tell well.